Exploring Leadership Styles and Faculty Satisfaction in Higher Education

Justin Bateh, D.B.A.

Author: **Justin Bateh, D.B.A.,** Jacksonville, FL
                 drbateh@gmail.com
                 www.drjustinbateh.com

Publisher: **DBC Publishing,** Virginia Beach, VA

Copyright ©   2013; 2016
ISBN Numbers   **IISBN-13: 978-0692757581**
                 ISBN-10: 0692757589

Disclaimer:

The author has attempted to gather as much of the facts and information to the utmost complete and truthfulness for the compilation of this book from bona fide sources, academic databases and libraries, personal interviews, Internet sources, printed material in currently circulating and non-circulating sources, and newspaper articles. Dates noted were from publically and privately available sources. Any data included (left out, incorrectly quoted, or attributed) may be attributed to transcription errors or types. Several bodies of research were interpretations of the same or original documents and errors might have occurred as transcribed.

Dr. Bateh's research interests are focused on the appropriate use of statistical methods and quantitative approaches to problems in organizational management and leadership, with a special focus on sustainable and socially responsible supply chains and operations. Any reader or researcher with more data to contribute to a future, updated, and corrected version of this project is encouraged to send materials to the researcher's email address noted on this page.

Please email drbateh@gmail.com if you are interested in collaborating on a research study of mutual interest.

Content and material in this book has been previously published in the following academic journal and copyrighted by JOLE:

Bateh, J., & Heyliger, W. (2014, July). Academic administrator leadership styles and the impact on faculty job satisfaction. *Journal of Leadership Education.* 13(*3*), 34-49. Retrieved from: http://www.journalofleadershiped.org/attach ments/article/351/13_3bateh201.pdf

INTRODUCTION

Universities must retain satisfied employees to enhance productivity and reduce turnover. Leadership represents one of the fundamental factors in job satisfaction. The purpose of this correlational study was to examine the relationship between perceived academic administrator leadership styles and the satisfaction of faculty members. The independent variables were the transformational, transactional, and passive/avoidant leadership styles of academic administrators as evaluated by faculty members. The dependent variable was job satisfaction of full-time faculty members. The Multifactor Leadership Questionnaire was used to identify the leadership style of an administrator as perceived by faculty members. Spector's Job Satisfaction Survey was used to assess a faculty member's level of job satisfaction. One hundred four participants from a state university in Florida completed the online survey. A logistic regression model was developed, and the statistically significant correlations indicated that (a) faculty members who identified transformational leadership as dominant had increased job satisfaction, (b) faculty members who identified transactional leadership as dominant had increased job satisfaction, and (c) faculty members who identified passive/avoidant leadership as dominant had decreased job satisfaction. Based on a 95% significance level, there was a significant relationship between the three leadership styles and job satisfaction. Using this model, academic leaders can take further action by refining their leadership styles on the basis of their faculty members' indicated preferences. The study results may contribute to social change by making academic administrators aware of effective leadership models that promote higher job satisfaction among faculty in universities.

TABLE OF CONTENTS

LIST OF TABLES

LIST OF FIGURES

CHAPTER 1
FOUNDATION OF THE STUDY

An organization's success depends on hiring and retaining satisfied employees (Cordeiro, 2010). Faculty members play a vital role in the success of higher education institutions (Cordeiro, 2010). Through increased job satisfaction, greater employee retention helps colleges and universities achieve adequate faculty allocations (Froeschle & Sinkford, 2009). Faculty job satisfaction and its relationship to retention in higher education are business-related issues, as a 5% increase in retention can lead to a 10% reduction in costs (Wong & Heng, 2009). A similar increase in retention can further result in substantial productivity increases, to as much as 65% (Wong & Heng, 2009).

Increased job satisfaction and better retention of faculty reduce the need for costly faculty selection and hiring, and higher retention adds financial stability to the institution (Froesche & Sinkford, 2009). Faculty members who remain with the institution for a long time develop experience and expertise that reduce the need for costly training of newly hired faculty members (Froesche & Sinkford, 2009). Finally, business professionals and entrepreneurs understand that truly sustainable advantage usually grows from innovations and creativity (Mutjaba, 2009).

The competition in the higher education sector is constantly changing, and higher education institutions cannot survive without retaining extraordinary faculty members who are innovative and creative (Mutjaba, 2009). Based on Mutjaba's argument, it appears that higher education institutions that have effective leadership procedures have a better likelihood of retaining high-quality faculty members, which may enable them to outperform their competitors and improve their financial standing. Therefore, my hypothesis for the present study relates to the argument that the relationship between academic administrator leadership styles and the job satisfaction of faculty members has a significant bearing on the academic and financial standing of higher education institutions. One such institution, specifically a Florida state university, is the focus of this study.

Background of the Problem

Universities in the United States experience high levels of faculty turnover (Klein & Takeda-Tinker, 2009). Most universities use faculty search committees that screen initial applications and, simultaneously, represent a massive investment of financial resources and faculty time (Cordeiro, 2010). The ability to hire and retain effective faculty remains a serious problem for higher education institutions (Wong & Heng, 2009). Job satisfaction plays a vital role in retaining faculty (Wong & Heng, 2009).

University leaders represent one of the fundamental factors in job satisfaction (Wong & Heng, 2009), and consequentially, they affect faculty turnover in higher education institutions. Faculty members often complain about the quality of institutional environments in which they operate; their intentions to leave relate to the quality of social relationships among them, other faculty members, and administrators (Wong & Heng, 2009). Most faculty members see their leaders and administrators as highly incompetent and lacking critical communication skills, and dissatisfaction with leadership

predisposes faculty members toward leaving their
positions (Klein & Takeda-Tinker, 2009).

Faculty member dissatisfaction with leadership in
higher education contrasts with the intellectual
satisfaction gained by faculty members. Faculty
members report enjoying a sense of professional
belonging when they develop satisfying collegial
relationships with peers (Klein & Takeda-Tinker, 2009).
While faculty members need the support of their leaders
to pursue projects requiring autonomy and
innovativeness, colleges and universities face the lack of
trained and qualified leaders who know how to assist
faculty members by providing the needed level of
support (Mutjaba, 2009).

Colleges and universities experience lack of
trained leaders for a number of reasons. As members of
the baby boomer population retire, which creates a
smaller workforce population, colleges draw new faculty
management members from a smaller pool of qualified
applicants (Campbell, Syed, & Morris, 2010; Finch,
Allen, & Weeks, 2010). Apart from the fact that hiring
and retaining talented college faculty leaders may be
extremely costly and time consuming (Green, Alejandro,
& Brown, 2009), generational differences play one of the

major roles in faculty members' continued dissatisfaction with leaders (Salahuddin, 2010). The difficulties seen in the State University System of Florida brings these generational difficulties to the surface. As the State University System of Florida is in the process of launching the New Florida Initiative, enrollments will likely increase across all universities within the system (State University System of Florida, 2012). This increased enrollment may result in rapid transformation of leadership positions because of the need for a larger teaching faculty (Lawrence & Bell, 2012). This may push administrators to assume new leadership responsibilities, and many leaders may not understand the importance of encouraging an open and productive conversation with faculty members (Lawrence & Bell, 2012)

Administrators selected for the new leadership positions may have little understanding of how their leadership decisions affect faculty members' satisfaction with their job (Klein & Takeda-Tinker, 2009). As faculty leaders retire, filling vacant faculty positions will also require much evaluation and thought. Research into a state university within the State University System of Florida, through the present study, may expose differences that exist between the motivations and desires of the academic leaders and faculty workers.

Problem Statement

Seventy-seven percent of employees in the United States have reported dissatisfaction with their jobs (Mardanov, Heischmidt, & Henson, 2008), and as DeConinck (2009) reported, job dissatisfaction eventually leads to voluntary turnover. The estimated salary premium required to replace one dissatisfied faculty member totals $57,000 (Finch et al., 2010). The general problem is that since the State University System of Florida launched the New Florida Initiative, increased enrollments created the need for faculty members to assume administrative positions with leadership responsibilities (Austin, 2012). Some new administrators lack knowledge of how their leadership style impacts faculty member job satisfaction (Lawrence & Bell, 2012). The specific business problem is the lack of a model for Florida university administrators to predict how leadership styles will impact job satisfaction of faculty members, and thus turnover rates.

Purpose Statement

The purpose of this quantitative correlational study was to examine the relationship between perceived academic administrator leadership styles and job satisfaction of full-time faculty members. The design of the study was correlational and nonexperimental. The independent variables were the transformational, transactional, and passive/avoidant leadership styles of academic administrators as evaluated by faculty members. The dependent variable was job satisfaction of full-time faculty members. The population consisted of 567 full-time faculty members within the university, including professors, associate professors, assistant professors, instructors, and lecturers (Bozeman & Guaghan, 2011). The minimum number of participants required for significant study results was 81, and 104 participated. The location of the study was an institution within the State University System of Florida, which had experienced increased demand for new leaders since the launch of the New Florida Initiative. The study results may contribute to social change by creating awareness of effective leadership models that promote higher job satisfaction in Florida universities.

Nature of the Study

Qualitative, quantitative, and mixed methods are the three methods used in research. Quantitative research methods examine the relationship between variables (Schweitzer, 2009). Additionally, quantitative methods rely on collecting and analyzing numerical data (Schweitzer, 2009). Qualitative research would not be appropriate to answer the research question because qualitative research enables a researcher to detect themes and to develop hypotheses, rather than to test hypotheses (Baxtor & Jack, 2008). Likewise, a mixed methods study that would incorporate a qualitative component along with the quantitative was not necessary, as the research questions and hypotheses would be best answered with quantitative data, which allows for generalization by making possible a much larger sample (Leech & Onwuegbuzie, 2011). The data for this study were numeric indicators of the variables of interest, and hence the study was quantitative. The method of data analysis was logistic regression – a form of regression appropriate for dependent variables measured on a binary scale – to test the primary hypotheses (Siemsen & Roth, 2010).

The researcher used a correlational design in this study because the quantitative data I collected from a large sample were more suited to this type of analysis (Schweitzer, 2009). The benefits of using a quantitative correlational approach are that the findings may generalize to the larger population of faculty members beyond the sample (Schweitzer, 2009). By using logistic regression as the primary analysis tool, this study design controlled for possible confounding variables (Siemsen & Roth, 2010).

Research Question

The researcher evaluated the relationship between academic administrator leadership styles and faculty job satisfaction within an institution in the State University System of Florida. Using the Multifactor Leadership Questionnaire (Bass & Avolio, 2012) and the Job Satisfaction Survey (Spector, 2011), the researcher sought to answer the following primary question and secondary research questions:

Primary Research Question 1: What is the relationship between perceived administrator leadership styles and job satisfaction of faculty members?

Secondary Research Question 2: What is the relationship between perceived transformational leadership styles and job satisfaction of faculty members?

Secondary Research Question 3: What is the relationship between perceived transactional leadership styles and job satisfaction of faculty members?

Secondary Research Question 4: What is the relationship between perceived passive/avoidant leadership styles and job satisfaction of faculty members?

Hypotheses

The researcher sought to answer the research questions by testing the following hypotheses:

$H1_o$: There is no significant relationship between leadership styles and job satisfaction of faculty members.

$H1_a$: There is a significant relationship between leadership styles and job satisfaction of faculty members.

H2o: There is no significant relationship between perceived transformational leadership styles and job satisfaction of faculty members.

H2a: There is a significant relationship between perceived transformational leadership styles and job satisfaction of faculty members.

H3o: There is no significant relationship between perceived transactional leadership styles and job satisfaction of faculty members.

H3a: There is a significant relationship between perceived transaction leadership styles and job satisfaction of faculty members.

H4o: There is no significant relationship between perceived passive/avoidant leadership styles and job satisfaction of faculty members.

H4a: There is a significant relationship between perceived passive/avoidant leadership styles and job satisfaction of faculty members.

Interview/Survey Questions

The survey questions originated from the Multifactor Leadership Questionnaire (MLQ 5X; Bass & Avolio, 2012), which is a quantitative survey and not a qualitative questionnaire, and Spector's Job Satisfaction Survey (2011).

Theoretical Framework

Relationships of leaders with their followers are extremely complicated. The path-goal theory of leadership remains one of the most popular theoretical frameworks explaining the process of leadership and leaders' interactions with followers. Robert J. House developed the theory; its principal meta-proposition is that effective leaders engage in behaviors that complement subordinates' environments and abilities (as cited in Northouse, 2010). By doing so, leaders compensate for the deficiencies of subordinates and heighten employee satisfaction as well as individual and work unit performance (Northouse, 2010).

The following are the main assumptions of path-goal theory: (a) path-goal theory is a theory regarding the supervisor-subordinate relationship (Northouse, 2010); (b) leader behaviors are acceptable and satisfying for subordinates as long as the leaders produce immediate satisfaction and create the foundation for future satisfaction in the subordinates

(Northouse, 2010); (c) leaders motivate their followers to the extent that they produce satisfaction among followers and complement the organizational environment by offering support, guidance, and rewards, when needed (Northouse, 2010); (d) situational characteristics such as the nature and complexity of task, the quality of the workplace environment, and the characteristics of followers predetermine the amount of time and effort leaders spend to improve subordinate performance and satisfaction (Yukl & Mahsud, 2010); and (e) leaders are effective only when they direct attention toward the needs and preferences of their subordinates, display concern for their subordinates' well-being, and can create and sustain a psychologically supportive and friendly work environment (Wang & Howell, 2012).

Vecchio, Justin, and Pearce (2008) used path-goal theory to explore the potential of transformational and transactional leadership models to predict performance satisfaction among followers. Fry and Kriger (2009) also mentioned path-goal theory as an example of a contingency approach to leadership, which focuses on finding the appropriate fit between a leader's behavior or style and the organizational conditions.

Contingency approaches focus on how leadership, subordinate characteristics, and situational elements influence one another (Northouse, 2010). Despite the paucity of the empirical literature, path-goal theory exemplifies a promising theoretical framework for the study of leaders' behaviors and their effects on job satisfaction among followers.

DEFINITION OF TERMS

The following list defines key terms used in the present study:

Passive/avoidant leadership style: For the purpose of the present study, this category includes two leadership styles: management by exception and laissez-faire leadership. In active leadership by exception, the leader monitors performance and acts only if it fails to meet the expected standards (Bass & Riggio, 2006). In passive management by exception, the leader waits for a problem to arise before taking action (Bass & Riggio, 2006). In the laissez-faire leadership style, the leader is less directly involved; he or she focuses only on the top-level issues while delegating the routine operations of the institution to subordinates (Simplicio, 2011).

Path-goal theory of leadership: Leader behaviors are acceptable and satisfying for subordinates as long as they produce immediate satisfaction and create the foundation for future satisfaction (Northouse, 2010). Leaders motivate their followers by offering support, guidance, and rewards, when needed (Northouse, 2010). Situational characteristics and the characteristics of followers predetermine the amount of time and effort leaders spend to improve subordinate performance and satisfaction (Yukl & Mahsud, 2010).

Transactional leadership: This style of leadership emphasizes smooth running of the organization by making sure (a) there is maintenance of the system and (b) there are clear goals. The leader puts emphasis on administrative issues and assesses the needs of subordinates to satisfy those needs in exchange for work. In essence, this model could qualify as "leadership by bartering" (Zembylas & Iasonos, 2010, p. 168).

Transformational leadership style: In this style, the leader actively works to shape the organizational culture by constructing a shared vision (Zembylas & Iasonos, 2010). The leader is charismatic and motivates employees through acting as a role model as well as providing inspirational motivation, intellectual stimulation, and individualized consideration (Zembylas & Iasonos, 2010, p. 372). Leaders value respect, autonomy, and the pursuit of higher goals (Bodla & Nawaz, 2010).

Assumptions, Limitations, and Delimitations

Assumptions

The researcher assumed participants would complete the survey in its entirety and with complete honesty. The researcher assumed the Florida state university studied represents and is typical of other universities in the State University System of Florida, especially in the area of the faculty members' and faculty leadership relations.

Limitations

The researcher sought to determine the relationship between perceived academic administrator leadership styles and full-time faculty job satisfaction within the State University System of Florida. Logistic regression allowed me to determine whether perceived leadership styles affected the probability of faculty members expressing satisfaction with their job. The coefficients from the logit models showed the size of the effect each independent variable has on the odds of job satisfaction, controlling for other potentially confounding variables such as demographics (Senter, 2012). I presented p-values alongside the coefficients to determine if the results of the effect size analysis were statistically significant. I used a significance level of .05. I used a two-tailed test for statistical significance. The study results may provide information regarding the relationship between leadership and job satisfaction. However, the possibility remained that the results of the study might not have correlated with job satisfaction.

Delimitations

The study sample included a single state university in the State University System of Florida out of 11 state universities. The study focused on academic administrators and full-time faculty at a specific public university, so the results of the study may not apply to 2-year community colleges or other 4-year state colleges. Furthermore, as the study sample included only a government-operated university, the results may not apply to for-profit, private colleges or universities, nor may the results apply to private sector corporations.

Significance of the Study

A study's potential to close the existing research and practice gaps usually depends upon the degree of a study's significance for practical application. In this chapter, the researcher discussed the significance of the present study for better understanding and practice of business and positive social change.

Reduction of Gaps

University administrators in the United States currently face high faculty turnover rates (Klein & Takeda-Tinker, 2009). Reasons why faculty members leave their jobs are numerous. Lack of institutional support and failure to keep up with one's discipline reduce organizational commitment and increase turnover intentions among faculty (Taylor & Berry, 2008). Administrators play a crucial role in the development of positive organizational cultures (Taylor & Berry, 2008). Contextual properties of educational institutions permit or impede the sense of belonging in faculty members (Xu, 2008a). Nonetheless, the relationship between job satisfaction and leadership styles of faculty administrators remains unclear. Administrators may use the results of this study to close the existing gap in the understanding of the effect of leadership style and improve faculty retention. The study meets the aim to measure the factors affecting job satisfaction of faculty members. The results are useful to enable faculty leaders to adjust their policies in ways that promote faculty member satisfaction with their jobs.

The academic administrators selected for leadership positions may not understand if their leadership style negatively affects faculty job satisfaction; in fact, academic administrators may not even be aware of their leadership style. This lack of understanding may be a serious business problem (Klein & Takeda-Tinker, 2009). However, researchers and policy makers assume that college administrators should develop collaborative ties. Administrators should also support and implement mentoring objectives for all faculty members (Fuller, Maniscalco-Feichtl, & Droege, 2008). The results of the study provide administrators with information that may guide their leadership decisions impacting their faculty, may lead them to improve and adjust their leadership styles, and consequentially, may result in faculty members' increased satisfaction with their jobs. This, in turn, will help higher education institutions reduce their costs by minimizing voluntary turnover and the costs of selection and training associated with turnover.

Implications for Social Change

Higher education is one of the central drivers of positive social change, and the quality of social progress directly depends upon the quality of higher education in the United States (Billiger & Wasilik, 2009). Faculty satisfaction is a complex construct that is difficult to predict, describe, and explain (Bolliger & Wasilik, 2009). Faculty members must perceive their teaching is effective for students and professionally beneficial for themselves (Bolliger & Wasilik, 2009). Increased job satisfaction should result in greater productivity (Froeschle & Sinkford, 2009). This, in turn, should expand the pool of educational resources provided by higher education institutions for positive social change.

Social change is impossible without talented leaders and inspired followers. The faculty is instrumental in the success of higher education (Bolliger & Wasilik, 2009). Great attention should be paid to faculty perceptions of both institutional and departmental leadership (Chung et al., 2010). At present, faculty dissatisfaction with leadership largely negates the intellectual satisfaction that could be gained from being part of higher education staff (Marston & Brunetti, 2009). The present study results can contribute to the development of effective leadership models in education and raises public awareness of the importance of effective leadership in public, state universities. This knowledge will enable higher education professionals to enhance their leadership decisions and, consequentially, drive positive social change.

A Review of the Professional
and Academic Literature

Leadership and job satisfaction are two of the most extensively studied areas in the quest to enhance human and organizational performance (Northouse, 2010). A substantial body of evidence supports the positive impact of transformational leadership on job satisfaction across occupational sectors (Northouse, 2010). Amidst sweeping waves of reforms in primary and secondary education, in the USA and internationally, transformational leadership emerged as the foremost leadership style, often explored in the context of teachers' job satisfaction and organizational culture and climate (Leithwood & Sun, 2012).

The literature review in this study came from the following EBSCO databases: Academic Search Premier, MasterFILE Premier, Business Source Premier, ERIC, PsycINFO, and PsycARTICLES. Keywords used either individually or in conjunction with other keywords included *colleges*, *universities*, *higher education*, *faculty*, *leadership*, *transformational leadership*, *transactional leadership*, *job satisfaction*, *work satisfaction*, *organizations*, *organizational commitment*, *turnover*, *autonomy*, *teaching*, *research*, *support*, *mentoring*, *governance*, *departments*, *academic*, and *disciplines*. The journals in which the articles appear span a wide range of scholarly and business disciplines. In the literature, I extensively reviewed the relationship between faculty job satisfaction and discovered that the leadership practices of administrators have gained less attention than business practice as a focus of research. Leadership style is typically one of a number of factors examined as a prospective source of faculty satisfaction or dissatisfaction (Klein & Takeda-Tinker, 2009). Specifically, faculty members' relationships with the department chair may play a prominent role in satisfaction (Klein & Takeda-Tinker, 2009).

The association between the job satisfaction and retention of college faculty members is more complicated than many have assumed. College faculty leaders must convey respect and recognition for professional expertise and autonomy, foster collegial relationships, and compensate faculty members fairly for the time and energy they invest in their work (Xu, 2008a). The implementation of effective practices is likely to bolster satisfaction and reduce turnover (Wong & Heng, 2009).

Because this study investigated the relationship between academic administrator leadership style and the job satisfaction of faculty at a Florida state university, the literature review included recognition of past studies' results on what factors lead to job satisfaction. Faculty members desire clear and reasonable expectations for performance and tenure, support for teaching,

professional development opportunities, autonomy,
opportunities for advancement, fair salary and benefits,
positive work-life balance, and a sense of collegiality
(Akroyd, 2011; Austin, 2012; Xu, 2008a). Faculty
members favor shared governance and involvement in
decision making (Lawrence & Bell, 2012). The
conditions that elicit faculty members' job satisfaction
and commitment and also those that provoke
dissatisfaction, and turnover intentions are under the
control of institutional leaders and amenable to change
(Lawrence & Bell, 2012). Job satisfaction is crucial for
the university because dealing with faculty turnover is
expensive (Cordeiro, 2010; Finch et al., 2010). There
are the financial costs of recruitment, hiring, and training
new faculty members, along with the time and energy
invested in the search, hiring, and socialization
processes (Cordeiro, 2010).

Contemporary Leadership Theories

**Transformational and transactional
leadership.** Comparison and contrast of
transformational and transactional leadership offer a
valuable perspective on leadership theory. Historically,
theories of leadership focused exclusively on the
characteristics of the leader (Bennis, 2010; Derue,
Nahrang, Wellman, & Humphrey, 2011; Yukl & Mahsud,
2010). According to Li and Hung (2009),
transformational leadership shifted the emphasis from
the leader to the quality of the relationship between
leaders and their followers. Li and Hung noted that
transformational leaders show similar values and
inspirational motivation. High-quality workplace
relationships are fundamental to positive work outcomes
(Li & Hung, 2009). Transformational leadership seems
to foster "the building and maintenance of social
networks in the workplace, and ... both vertical and
lateral forms of social ties help facilitate employees'
higher levels of task performance and active
participation in citizenship behaviors" (Li & Hung, 2009,
p. 1141). Invoking Maslow's hierarchy of needs, Bass

and Riggio (2006) pointed out that transactional leaders secure and maintain power by focusing on their followers' lower order needs while transformational leaders encourage their followers toward self-realization. In contrast, transactional leadership puts emphasis on administrative issues and assesses the needs of subordinates to satisfy those needs in exchange for work (Zembylas & Iasonos, 2010).

Comparison and contrast of transformational and transactional leadership often lead to preference for one over the other, but not always. Bass and Riggio (2006) recognized that the most effective leaders use both transformational and transactional leadership. In fact, Yukl and Mahsud (2010) decried the dualistic approaches to leadership that emerged during the 20th Century, such as the juxtaposition of task-oriented and relationship-oriented leadership and transformational and transactional leadership. Yukl and Mahsud considered the ability to be versatile and adapt one's leadership style to the demands of the situation to be a hallmark of an effective leader. Bass and Riggio's model of transformational leadership has undergone many changes since its inception in the 1980s. This model meets the criteria of a full-range model, spanning

transformational, transactional, and laissez-faire
leadership styles (Bass & Riggio, 2006).

The four-I model provides the basis for
transformational leadership (Bass & Riggio, 2006). Bass
and Riggio (2006) noted this model includes four main
aspects: idealized influence (or charisma), inspirational
motivation, individualized consideration, and intellectual
stimulation. Bass and Riggio stated that *idealized
influence* refers to behaviors that elicit respect,
admiration, and trust from followers. This aspect of
transformational leadership includes leadership by
example, which the principal *modeling the way*
embodies as described in the *Five Practices of
Exemplary Leadership* (Kouzes & Posner, 2007).
Supporting these findings, Deluga (2011) collected
survey data from 86 subordinate-supervisor groups
employed in a variety of organizations. He found
perceived fairness emerged as the supervisor trust-
building behavior most closely associated with desired
organizational citizenship behaviors in subordinates.
Inspirational motivation refers to the ability to
communicate a compelling vision that spurs action
toward individual and collective goals (Bass & Riggio,
2006). Bass and Riggio stated that leaders who practice

intellectual stimulation seek ideas, opinions, and input from their followers to promote creativity, innovation, and experimentation. Bass and Riggio also asserted *individualized consideration* involves actively listening and being sensitive to each person's needs for growth, learning, and recognition.

The Multifactor Leadership Questionnaire (MLQ) captures the full range of leader behaviors, which include those that distinguish between transformational leadership, transactional leadership, and laissez-faire leadership (Bass & Riggio, 2006). Bass and Riggio's (2006) factor analysis of the MLQ showed significant correlations between individualized consideration and transactional contingent reward leadership. Transactional leadership can serve as a foundation for building transformational leadership (Bass & Riggio, 2006). Bass and Riggio also stated contingent reward leadership molds expectations for performance and fairness and works to build trust between the leader and followers. Contingent reward is implicit in the role of fair and competitive salary and compensation in the satisfaction of college faculty (Bass & Riggio, 2006).

Researchers such as Rowold and Scholtz (2009) and Lenhardt, Ricketts, Morgan, and Karnock (2011) have studied the MLQ alone or in conjunction with the Leadership Practices Inventory (LPI). Rowold and Schlotz, using the MLQ, found transformational leadership to relate to job satisfaction. Similarly, Lenhardt et al. found statistically significant results of transformational leadership relating to job satisfaction using the LPI and MLQ. Lenhardt et al. concluded that increasing transformational leadership behaviors would likely result in positive employee outcomes, which would produce "benefits including a more enduring and meaningful working relationship between a superintendent and his or her employees, potential cost savings, and financial benefits from an increase in employee performance, and employee retention" (p. 29).

Passive leadership. Two types of leadership contrast with descriptions of both transactional and transformational leadership (Bass & Riggio, 2006). Bass and Riggio (2006) stated that in active leadership by exception, the leader monitors performance. In other words, the leader acts only if the performance fails to meet the expected standards. Bass and Riggio also stated that in passive management by exception, the leader waits for a problem to arise before taking action.

Laissez-faire leadership essentially means the absence of leadership (Bass & Riggio, 2006). Researchers reviewed by Bass and Riggio found less effective results with management by exception and laissez-faire leadership. The less effective modes of leadership are far less common than transformational and transactional contingent reward leadership (Bass & Riggio, 2006).

Individualized consideration distinguishes authentic transformational leaders from pseudo-transformational leaders (Bass & Riggio, 2006). In a study of teachers from high-performing schools, Leithwood and Sun (2012) observed a relationship between the principals' use of individualized consideration and the importance the teachers ascribed to a collegial, professional climate. A similar relationship appears throughout the literature on college faculty job satisfaction (Klein & Takeda-Tinker, 2009). Some theorists approach individualized consideration from the perspectives of developmental leadership and supportive leadership (Wang & Howell, 2012). Wang and Howell (2012) examined the effects of supportive and developmental leadership on employees. Wang and Howell defined supportive leadership as taking place when leaders express concern for followers' needs and preferences and take account of these needs and preferences when making decisions.

Supportive leadership can effectively buffer against job stress (Wang & Howell, 2012). This aspect of supportive leadership (or individualized consideration) may be especially valuable for faculty members under conditions of organizational change (Coates, Dobson, Goedegebuure, & Meek, 2010). The behaviors associated with supportive leadership overlap heavily with mentoring, which faculty early in their careers strongly desire (Austin, 2012).

Both supportive and developmental leadership convey the message that the leader cares for the well-being of followers, and both leadership types have positive effects (Wang & Howell, 2012). However, Wang and Howell (2012) observed a strong effect for developmental leadership on affective commitment, career certainty, job satisfaction, and the confidence to perform tasks outside the usual scope of one's job. Of the two types of leadership, developmental leadership may align more closely with transformational leadership (Wang & Howell, 2012). Both developmental, and supportive leadership, particularly on the part of the department chair, may have a significant impact on faculty members (Wang & Howell, 2012).

The Leadership Practices Inventory

Unlike the MLQ, which spans the full range of
leadership behaviors (Muenjohn & Armstrong, 2008), the
Leadership Practices Inventory focuses on
transformational leadership (Gill, 2011; Kouzes &
Posner, 2007). The 30-item LPI assesses the Five
Practices of Exemplary Leadership (Kouzes & Posner,
2007). The qualities embedded in the five practices
stem from over 25 years of research by Kouzes and
Posner (2007). Kouzes and Posner studied qualities
exhibited by managers in a wide variety of industry and
organizational settings in the United States and abroad.
These five practices, as noted by Kouzes and Posner,
are (a) modeling the way, (b) inspiring a shared vision,
(c) enabling others to act, (d) challenging the process,
and (e) encouraging the heart. Modeling the way
embodies the concept of leadership by example,
meaning the actions of exemplary leaders are congruent
with their words (Kouzes & Posner, 2007). Leaders
enable others to act; thus, they promote teamwork,
collaboration, and empowerment (Kouzes & Posner,

2007). Challenging the process can be construed as leadership for change (Kouzes & Posner, 2007). Leaders who encourage new ideas and novel solutions to problems are those who challenge, seek new opportunities, support creativity, and support innovation (Kouzes & Posner, 2007). Encouraging the heart means that leaders foster involvement by recognizing and rewarding personal contributions and celebrating achievements (Kouzes & Posner, 2007). Recognition for their contribution to the institution is of paramount concern to faculty members (Kouzes & Posner, 2007). Enabling is the most prevalent of the five practices, while inspiring is the most difficult (Kouzes & Posner, 2007).

Use of the LPI offers the advantage of comparison with and validation by a substantial amount of past research. Stout-Stewart (2005) used the LPI in a study of female community college presidents. In addition, Castro (as cited in Derue et al., 2011) used the LPI in a study involving chief academic officers (CAOs), undergraduate deans, and academic department chairs. Using the LPI, Klein and Takeda-Tinker (2009) studied faculty member satisfaction with business faculty leadership. However, there has been some criticism of these studies by Jing and Avery (2011). The prior use of this measure for faculty leadership minimizes problems related to Jing and Avery's criticism. Jing and Avery observed that the hypothesized leadership-performance relationship suggested by past researchers led to inconclusive findings and difficulty in interpreting the results. Jing and Avery also noted that the many different concepts of leadership employed in different studies make direct comparisons virtually impossible.

Path-Goal Theory

Robert J. House and his colleagues developed the path-goal theory in an attempt to resolve inconsistent and paradoxical findings arising from Fiedler's contingency theory (Northouse, 2010). The contingency theory (a) classified leaders as either task motivated or relationship motivated and (b) indicated that leadership motivation is a relatively fixed and stable characteristic (Northouse, 2010; Vecchio et al., 2008). According to path-goal theory, the leader's role is to create and manage followers' paths toward individual and collective goals, clarify expectations, and enrich the environment when the existing rewards are inadequate (Vecchio et al., 2008). The effects of leadership traits, such as consideration, initiating structure, achievement-oriented leadership, and participative leadership likely depend on contingency factors related to follower characteristics and environmental features (Vecchio et al., 2008). Acceptance of the leadership, work satisfaction, and investment of effort in high performance result from a good match between the leader's actions and the situation (Fry & Kriger, 2009).

Although path-goal leadership first appeared in 1970, preceding transformational leadership, it has been the subject of far less research (Vecchio et al., 2008). House recently presented a model linking path-goal theory to certain aspects of transformational leadership (as cited in Vecchio et al., 2008). According to the model, leaders exercise transactional contingent reward leadership by gaining influence through the use of external incentives that are contingent on followers' performance (Vecchio et al., 2008). In situations absent the use of extrinsic rewards, the model predicts enhanced impact of transformational leadership (Vecchio et al., 2008). House theorized that articulating a vision, conveying high performance expectations, and providing frequent positive feedback would be especially pertinent to the interaction of path-goal theory and transformational leadership (as cited in Vecchio et al., 2008).

The path-goal theory revealed key aspects of existing theories. Vecchio et al. (2008) tested House's theory in a study of 179 high school teachers and their principals. The findings showed the leader's vision and intellectual stimulation had greater influence in situations with limited use of contingent reward (Vecchio et al., 2008). A notable finding was that transactional leadership had more influence on performance than anticipated (Vecchio et al., 2008). In fact, the influence of transactional leadership surpassed the influence of transformational leadership (Vecchio et al., 2008). Nonetheless, the findings suggested transactional leadership might have more potential for explaining performance outcomes than other researchers had recognized (Vecchio et al., 2008).

Another study also revealed complex affects regarding transactional and transformational leadership (Pieterse, van Knippenberg, Schippers, & Stam, 2009). Pieterse et al. (2009) proposed that follower psychological empowerment moderates the relationship of leadership type and follower innovative behavior. Pieterse et al. conducted a field study with 230 employees of a government agency. The results showed that when psychological empowerment was high, transformational leadership positively correlated with innovative behavior, whereas transactional leadership negatively correlated with innovative behavior under the same condition (Pieterse et al., 2009).

College and University Presidents

College presidents vary tremendously in their leadership styles, but they all share the common characteristic of being "the most powerful individual on their respective campuses" (Simplicio, 2011, p. 110). Their mode of governance plays a pivotal role in the life of the institution and its human capital (Simplicio, 2011, p. 110). Simplicio (2011) outlined several styles of leadership in academia, ranging from democratic to tyrannical. The democratic leader favors shared governance, involving others in decision-making and encouraging feedback, creativity, and innovation (Simplicio, 2011, p. 110). Shared governance imbues members of the institution with a sense of pride and ownership, which in turn stimulates enthusiasm, energy, and motivation (Lawrence & Bell, 2012). Driven by a shared vision, individuals within a shared governance system show willingness to exert extra effort to work toward collective goals (Tinberg, 2009). A democratic system promotes personal and professional growth, and throughout the organization, members welcome new ideas and change (Lawrence & Bell, 2012).

While most leadership styles have strengths that positively affect a variety of situations, there are other undesirable styles, such as the laissez-faire leadership style (Simplicio, 2011). Laissez-faire is almost invariably the least effective mode of leadership (Bass & Riggio, 2006). Simplicio (2011) did not see laissez-faire as entirely ineffective on a college campus. Rather, Simplicio described the laissez-faire college president as one who focuses only on the top-level issues while delegating the routine operations of the institution to subordinates. Managers such as department chairs, deans, and directors show expertise in their respective fields and, therefore, may be excellent leaders and decision makers within their scope of influence (Simplicio, 2011). However, Simplicio states that the laissez-faire college presidents fail to retain a current understanding of what is happening on campus and, perhaps most importantly, the people who comprise the organization. Leadership authors almost universally deride another style of leadership, the autocratic style (Simplicio, 2011). This leader micro-manages and attempts to run all aspects of the institution (Simplicio, 2011). Autocratic leadership depresses creativity and innovation and thus is antithetical to intellectual stimulation (Bass & Riggio, 2006). An exaggeration of an autocratic leader is the tyrannical leader who often governs through fear (Simplicio, 2011). While leaders who insist they must be the ultimate authority on all matters are extremely ineffective, they have not disappeared entirely from the landscape of higher education (Simplicio, 2011). The autocratic leader rigidly relies on rules, policies, and protocols, and the institution is likely to be in a state of stagnation (Simplicio, 2011).

The charismatic leadership style elicits both praise and caution (Bass & Riggio, 2006). Charisma constitutes an essential component of transformational leadership, however, critics such as Bass and Riggio (2006) stated that charismatic leadership fosters dependency in followers. Authentic transformational leadership has the power to help followers realize their own sense of leadership (Bass & Riggio, 2006). Transformational leadership propels followers toward growth and development, not dependency (Bass & Riggio, 2006).

The LPI results present practical and realistic leadership solutions. Utilizing the LPI, Stout-Stewart (2005) explored the attitudes and behaviors of 126 female, community college presidents. These presidents represented a broad range of institutions situated in rural, urban, and suburban communities (Stout-Stewart, 2005). Relatively few participants headed urban institutions; however, geographic locale had no impact on leadership style (Stout-Stewart, 2005). The participants were primarily Caucasian and the overwhelming majority held doctoral degrees (Stout-Stewart, 2005). As a group, the doctoral degree holders outperformed their colleagues with Master's degrees on the five leadership practices (Stout-Stewart, 2005).

In descending order, the commonest leadership practices were enabling others to act, modeling the way, encouraging the heart, challenging the process, and inspiring a shared vision (Stout-Stewart, 2005). Kouzes and Posner (2007) presented enabling as the most prevalent leadership practice. Enabling involves the exercise of concrete actions that promote self-confidence, independence, and self-direction (Kouzes &

Posner, 2007). On the other hand, many leaders are less confident in their ability to inspire (Kouzes & Posner, 2007). The use of encouraging the heart is positive in view of the desire of faculty members for recognition and the dissatisfaction caused by lack of appreciation for exemplary performance (Houston et al., 2006).

Past research has focused on the prevalence of leadership styles among administrators in higher education according to race or ethnicity. An intriguing finding was that Latina, Asian, and Native American presidents engaged in encouraging the heart and inspiring a shared vision more than either African American or Caucasian presidents, though the African American presidents scored higher on both measures than their Caucasian counterparts (Stout-Stewart, 2005). These differences illustrated the role of culture in leadership styles and perhaps the interplay of gender and culture (Ayman & Korabik, 2010). Stout-Stewart (2005) also examined the prospective role of student enrollment patterns on the community college presidents' leadership practices. Stout-Stewart also found that while total enrollment had no significant impact, the proportion of full-time students influenced the practices of inspiring, enabling, and encouraging. As a group, the presidents were above average in their use of the five practices (Stout-Stewart, 2005).

Much past research has focused on the prevalence of leadership styles among administrators in higher education according to gender. Stout-Stewart (2005) suggested that women may be more inclined than men toward transformational and participative leadership styles. Ayman and Korabik (2010) presented some evidence for that claim; however, findings vary according to the situation. The leadership practices of the female, community college presidents may symbolize a trend away from the hierarchical structure that has traditionally defined public 2-year institutions (Ayman & Korabik, 2010). Instead, female leadership tends toward a shared governance model (Jenkins & Jensen, 2010).

Webb (2009) explored the leadership behaviors of top executives of 104 colleges and universities that are members of the Council for Christian Colleges and Universities (CCCU). The positions held by the respondents in Webb's study included provost, vice president of academic affairs, vice president of business or financial affairs, vice president or dean of student affairs, executive vice president, and several other executive positions. The instrument used in Webb's study was the MLQ 5X-short. Regarding the college executives' leadership styles, the pattern that emerged aligns with Bass and Riggio's (2006) model of effective leadership.

In other words, transformational leadership was the most prevalent leadership style, followed by transactional contingent reward leadership, active management by exception, passive management by exception, and laissez-faire leadership (Webb, 2009). Webb found that leaders exercised the three passive modes of leadership to a much lesser degree than the more active and effective leadership styles. Individual influence (behavioral idealized influence) was the most prevalent form of transformational leadership, although it was only slightly more common than inspirational motivation and attributed charisma (Webb, 2009).

Other past research focused on the prevalence of leadership styles among administrators in higher education according to the effectiveness of the styles. As interpreted by Webb (2009), employees were most likely to be motivated and willing to exert extra effort by a leader who displays self-confidence, energy, personal conviction, assertiveness and power, or in a word, charisma. Intellectual stimulation, individualized consideration, and contingent reward leadership all work together beyond the leader's charisma to create an exciting and energizing work environment (Webb, 2009). The importance of having a fair reward and incentive system cannot be downgraded, and indeed it is essential to building trust (Bass & Riggio, 2006).

Laissez-faire and both active and passive management by exception diminished the drive to invest extra effort in work (Bass & Riggio, 2006). Simplicio (2011) noted laissez-faire leaders lose touch with their employees. As Simplicio also stated, not only do they not provide feedback and encouragement, but their lack of involvement may make staff members feel that the university leadership does not value them personally or professionally. The strongly positive impact of the leader's charisma on motivation highlights the powerful influence of modeling on behavior (Simplicio, 2011). It seems intuitive that a highly energetic, confident, and enthusiastic leader would inspire the same feelings in others to the advantage of their productivity and performance (Simplicio, 2011).

Much past leadership research focused on the effectiveness of skills and traits. The study by Webb

(2009) focused on the leadership behaviors of college and university presidents and their impact on employee job satisfaction. In this study, Webb noted college presidents need to possess strong leadership and managerial skills. Planning, fundraising, and budgeting are intrinsic to the position of the college president, and these tasks require the vision, influence, and strong interpersonal skills of an excellent leader (Webb, 2009). The participants were overwhelmingly Caucasian (97%) and male (8.16%), with an average age of about 50 years and an average of 7.14 years in their present position, as noted by Webb.

Attributed charisma emerged as the leadership quality that accounted for the greatest degree of variance in job satisfaction (Webb, 2009). Webb also noted that effects of the other leadership behaviors were minimal by comparison. Contingent reward and individualized consideration, along with attributed charisma, explained the variation in job satisfaction (Webb, 2009). There was a substantial degree of an interrelationship between contingent reward leadership and transformational leadership, which is not unusual (Bass & Riggio, 2006).

Leadership for Diversity

In exploring college presidents' transformational and transactional leadership styles as they work to promote diversity agendas on campus, Kezar (2010) found compelling support for the effectiveness of a wide range of leadership behaviors. Most of the presidents saw idealized influence as a powerful force for advancing the diversity agenda, especially in the early stages (Kezar, 2010). Presidents exhibiting leadership by example made a persuasive case for the diversity agenda (Kezar, 2010). Kezar concluded that engaging in ongoing dialogue with the students was a pivotal facet of transformational leadership. Individual consideration gained importance in the mid-stages of the diversity project (Kezar, 2010).

Interestingly, a majority of the college presidents of color felt they could advance the diversity agenda effectively by exercising transactional leadership (Kezar, 2010). Kezar (2010) emphasized the presidents of color were quite capable of transformational leader behaviors. Kezar assessed the campus diversity climate and perceived that transactional leadership was a superior

strategy for achieving their objectives. When presidents
engaged in transformational leadership, the leaders of
color felt it was essential to have the support of key
stakeholders (such as the board) who would publicly
express their commitment to the diversity agenda
(Kezar, 2010). All of the presidents attuned themselves
to the perceptions of their constituents, which guided
their approach to advancing the diversity agenda (Kezar,
2010).

Deans and Department Chairs' Leadership Styles

Much valuable research has emerged from the
focus on levels of leadership among administrators in
higher education in relation to leadership style. Castro
(as cited in Derue et al., 2011) selected the LPI and the
Emotional Competence Inventory (ECI) for a study of the
leadership practices of CAOs, undergraduate deans,
and academic department chairs from 12 Carnegie I
research institutions. The deans surpassed the
department chairs on all five leadership practices and
the CAOs on all practices with the exception of modeling
the way, though the differences did not reach statistical
significance in Derue et al.'s (2011) study. Similarly, the

deans emerged as the most emotionally competent of the three groups of leaders (Derue et al., 2011). There were significantly positive interrelationships between the five practices and emotional self-awareness (Derue et al., 2011). Several traits related to achievement orientation: challenging the heart, inspiring a shared vision, enabling others to act, and encouraging the heart (Derue et al., 2011). On the other hand, several traits related to developing others: challenging the process, inspiring a shared vision, modeling the way, and encouraging the heart (Derue et al., 2011). There is a relationship between transformational leadership and emotional competence (Derue et al., 2011).

Department chairs have predictable duties. In the performance of these duties, chairpersons must perform four essential roles: leader, scholar, faculty developer, and manager (Petersen & Caplow, 2004). Petersen and Caplow (2004) investigated the influence of department chairs' leadership and communication styles on their effectiveness as perceived by faculty members. The instruments Petersen and Caplow chose were the Path-Goal Leadership Questionnaire, the Norton Communication Style Instrument, and the Department Chair Role Orientation Instrument. The respondents to

Petersen and Caplow's online survey were 86 faculty members drawn from 65 leadership higher education programs. The information on faculty interactions produced four leadership styles: *directive, supportive, participative*, and *achievement-oriented,* according to Petersen and Caplow. The descriptions of the chairs' communication styles included friendly, impression-leaving, relaxed, contentious or argumentative, attentive, precise, animated and expressive, dramatic, open, and dominant (Petersen & Caplow, 2004).

The same study examined the prevalence of leadership style among chairpersons. The most common leadership style appeared as achievement-oriented, followed by directive and participative (Petersen & Caplow, 2004). No department chairs characterized themselves as displaying a supportive leadership style (Petersen & Caplow, 2004). The faculty members viewed achievement-oriented and directive chairs as the most effective (Petersen & Caplow, 2004). In view of this preference, Peterson and Caplow (2004) stated that it is not unexpected that most respondents viewed their chairs as exhibiting a dominant communication style. Petersen and Caplow equated this style with being clear and articulate, which is inherently effective. Demographic characteristics did not influence the chairs' leadership or communication styles in Petersen and Caplow's study. Despite the limited use of supportive leadership, the faculty members enjoyed a substantial degree of autonomy (Petersen & Caplow, 2004). Academic faculty place more importance on their professional autonomy than their relationships with administrators and prefer administrators who respect their independence and freedom (Marston & Brunetti, 2009).

Related research has focused on leadership style prevalence among administrators in higher education based on the size of the department. For example, Whitsett utilized the Leadership Effectiveness and Adaptability Description (LEAD) and a Personal Information Data Sheet to examine leadership styles among the department chairs at a small private university (as cited in Petersen & Caplow, 2004). Whitsett chose as respondents 64 faculty members and seven department chairs (as cited in Petersen & Caplow, 2004). Whitsett chose leadership styles covered by the LEAD: *telling, selling, participating,* and *delegating* (as cited in Petersen & Caplow, 2004). The predominant leadership style (reported by both chairs and faculty in

Whitsett's study) was selling, a style in which the leader seeks to get faculty to accept and execute desired behaviors (Petersen & Caplow, 2004). Similarly, Sirkipes (2011) observed that the size of the department affected the chairs' behavior, with the heads of smaller departments preferring a participative leadership style. Pragmatically, it may be easier to manage participative leadership in a smaller department (Sirkipes, 2011). From that standpoint, the department chairs may be selecting a leadership style they find most appropriate for their situation, which is a characteristic of an effective leader (Yukl & Mahsud, 2010). Their profiles indicated the department chairs had a moderate degree of adaptability (Sirkis, 2011).

Some past research emphasized the effects of mentoring as a leadership style or attribute. In a study of nursing faculty by Gutierrez, Candela, and Carver (2012), the faculty members' perceived organizational support, developmental experiences, person-organization fit, and global job satisfaction positively predicted their organizational commitment. Guttierrez et al. (2012) also found that the faculty administrators who used mentoring skills were able to build positive relationships with nursing faculty, which in turn, led to increased organizational commitment, productivity, job satisfaction, and perceived organizational support.

Other research focused on the prevalence of certain leadership styles among administrators in higher education, based on chairperson demographic characteristics. Jones and Rudd (2008) explored the use of transformational, transactional, and laissez-faire leadership by academic deans or program directors in colleges of agriculture and life sciences at land grant universities. A total of 56 academic leaders responded to Jones and Rudd's survey. As a group, the deans in Jones and Rudd's survey tended to prefer transformational leadership, also making use of transactional leadership. Reliance on laissez-faire leadership was minimal (Jones & Rudd, 2008). For all three types of leadership behaviors, the male academic leaders had higher scores than their female colleagues (Jones & Rudd, 2008). This finding by Ayman and Korabik (2010) contradicts the prior research by Jones and Rudd that reported women as more disposed than men toward transformational leadership. Ethnic minority leaders displayed more transformational and transactional leadership behaviors than Caucasian academic leaders in the study by Jones and Rudd.

The overall pattern was, irrespective of gender or ethnicity; the academic leaders made effective use of transformational and transactional leadership (Jones & Rudd, 2008)

Faculty Job Satisfaction

Teaching in higher education requires a considerable amount of diligence and commitment, as well as much unsupervised work. As a result, vital characteristics of faculty members include mental commitment and loyalty, rather than only physical presence (Rashid, & Rashid, 2011).

Perceived unwritten contract. Faculty member satisfaction relies partially on the university meeting their end of an unwritten contract as faculty members fulfill their perceived obligations to the university (Rashid, & Rashid, 2011). Krivokapic-Skoko and O'Neill's (2008) study reinforced the importance of leadership and management showing fairness and equity in relation to the promotion and provision of opportunities for career development. The academics' perceived obligations to the university, in turn, relates to the importance of meeting role expectations, commitment to the job, and student learning (Krivokapic-Skoko & O'Neill, 2008).

Changing Academic Profession Survey.

Higher education faced rapid changes during the past decade, according to results tracked by the Changing Academic Profession Survey (CAPS). The Changing Academic Profession Survey began in 2007 with 19 countries and has continued to expand (Coates et al., 2010). The survey encompassed salaries, job satisfaction, propensity to change jobs, research opportunities, contract conditions, workload, environmental support, and leadership (Coates et al., 2010). Coates et al. (2010) presented the findings with emphasis on perceptions of Australian faculty members toward their universities' leadership and compared them to other countries. The study results illuminated the perceptions of American faculty (Coates et al., 2010). The ambitious CAPS project provides a complete overview for examining faculty job satisfaction and views of leadership in greater detail (Coates et al., 2010).

Administrators exert a substantial influence on the culture and environment of higher education faculty. Coates et al. (2010) stated succinctly, "The environment in which academics work is critical to their perceptions of the job" (p. 381). By extension, the president sets the tone for that environment (Simplicio, 2011). The charted responses in the Coates et al.'s study covered the following issues:

- Faculty members' personal influence in working to shape key academic policies at levels ranging from the department to the institution;
- The degree to which top administrators provide competent leadership;
- How well the university kept faculty members informed about what happens at the institution;
- Problems with lack of academic staff involvement;
- Whether students should have a stronger voice in policies affecting them;
- Whether the administration supports academic freedom.

As an extension of the research on the culture and environment of higher education faculty, further research focused on job satisfaction for higher education faculty based on position level. The Australian academics' satisfaction with leadership not only fell

below average, but only the British and Hong Kong
faculty scored lower than the Australians (Coates et al.,
2010). In contrast, Coates et al. (2010) found that
United States-based faculties were at the higher end of
the spectrum. For almost all the countries, the levels of
satisfaction paralleled the faculty ranks, with senior
faculty members expressing the highest satisfaction,
followed by middle and then junior faculty members
(Coates et al., 2010). Coates et al. found that faculty
members from China, Mexico, and Malaysia expressed
the highest overall levels of satisfaction with leadership.
Coates et al.'s most striking finding was that, of all the
countries, the gap between the satisfaction of senior and
junior faculty members was the most pronounced in the
United States. The pattern for the Australian academics
was not remarkably different (Coates et al., 2010).

Characteristics of the culture and environment of
higher education faculty lead to dissatisfaction. To
assess institutional support, Coates et al. (2010) asked
respondents a broad question. The researchers asked
whether conditions in higher education and research
institutions had improved or declined since they began
their career, which preceded questions specific to their
institution (Coates et al., 2010). The questions designed

by Coates et al. asked whether the institution had the following characteristics: (a) good communication between management and faculty, (b) a top-down management style, (c) collegial decision making processes, (d) a strong performance orientation, (e) a cumbersome administrative process, (f) a supportive attitude on the part of administrative staff toward teaching activities, (g) a supportive attitude on the part of administrative staff toward research, and (h) professional development for administrative or management activities for individual faculty members.

On a scale of 4.0, the perceptions of support by United Stages-based faculty were just under 3.0, one of the highest scores in the Coates et al. study. Thus among the countries the U.S. academics were fairly well satisfied with institutional support and top management (Coates et al., 2010).

The same study also considered international differences in faculty satisfaction (Coates et al., 2010). The United States-based academics were also among the most satisfied with the features of their institutional facilities, surpassed only by faculty from Finland, Hong Kong, and Germany (Coates et al., 2010). For institutional support, only Malaysia, China, Korea, and

Mexico were higher, although the difference between the United States and Mexico was negligible (Coates et al., 2010). The only troubling finding in the Coates et al. study was the marked gap in satisfaction between senior, middle, and junior faculty in American higher education. Coates et al. attributed the low satisfaction of the Australian and U.K. faculty members to the fact that higher education systems have, in the past decade, gone through massive changes to an unprecedented degree. Only China has experienced a comparable degree of change (Coates et al., 2010). Yet the changes have produced markedly divergent results; Chinese academics have the highest level of satisfaction with leadership and the second highest satisfaction with institutional support (Coates et al., 2010). Coates et al., in response to the contrasting patterns, raised the question of how changes at the institutional and department levels might affect the perceptions of faculty members. In the United States, the inequities in power and influence that affect the satisfaction with institutional leadership of faculty members at different levels should serve as a springboard for positive organizational change (Coates et al., 2010).

Academic faculty. Qualitative studies offer
another avenue for investigation of job satisfaction for
academic faculty. Ambrose, Huston and Norman's
(2005) qualitative study intended to delve beyond the
information produced by a fixed-response survey. A
unique feature of the study is that researchers matched
current faculty members with former faculty from the
same university (Ambrose et al., 2005). Where possible,
researchers matched the two groups by gender and race
(Ambrose et al., 2005). Most of the former faculty
members in the study had left their positions voluntarily
(Ambrose et al., 2005). Most were still academics, and
most had gained tenured at their new university
(Ambrose et al., 2005). The 62 current faculty members
included 42 tenured professors (Ambrose et al., 2005).
Contrary to the presumed relationship between job
satisfaction and retention, virtually identical proportions
of former and current faculty members reported
satisfaction with the university (54% and 53%,
respectively), noted Xu (2008a). The proportion of
former faculty who described their experience as
negative was only slightly higher than that for the current
faculty (43% and 39%), noted Xu. However, Ambrose et
al. (2005) discovered participants' detailed descriptions

of their experiences were often incongruent with their overall assessments.

The factors underlying the participants' satisfaction or dissatisfaction fell into seven broad categories in Ambrose's study (Ambrose et al., 2005). Five customarily found in the literature include the following: salaries, mentoring, collegiality, reappointment, promotion and tenure, and department chairs (Ambrose et al., 2005). The other two categories, which related to regional issues and the interdisciplinary focus of the university, emerged as more unique to the setting than these five stated categories (Ambrose et al., 2005).

Both tangible and intangible incentives motivate faculty members. One study used a concept from Matier's earlier research describing *internal benefits* and *external benefits* (Ambrose et al., 2005). Internal benefits encompass intangible features such as autonomy, influence, sense of belonging, and institutional and personal reputation, along with tangible benefits such as salary and fringe benefits, facilities, and policy (Xu, 2008a). External benefits fall outside the realm of work. External benefits include family, friends, quality of life, and financial issues beyond salary (Xu,

2008a).   Ambrose et al. (2005) noted internal factors as significant in the decision to stay or leave while external benefits were not significant in that decision. However, the fusion of low-internal benefits at the institution, expectations for high-internal benefits elsewhere, and the freedom to leave is likely to spur the decision to leave the institution (Xu, 2008a).

As a relevant extension of internal and external benefits, Xu (2008a) connected these benefits to faculty retention efforts. According to Xu, some faculty members described low external benefits. Examples of external benefits listed by Xu include helping faculty members find suitable housing, assisting their partners or spouses in finding jobs, and helping new faculty members feel less socially or culturally isolated. Though these pose a challenge for the institution to address, external benefits can be especially helpful for faculty members relocating to the area, especially when entering from another country and culture (Xu, 2008a). According to Xu, taking steps to improve the internal benefits for faculty members is certainly under the institution's control. As Xu observed, most of the sources of satisfaction and dissatisfaction are common and are amenable to change by institutional leadership.

Further, Xu suggested the need to pay attention to discipline-specific patterns in future studies of faculty turnover behaviors. Administrators need to realize that retention efforts should go beyond general human resources issues. Xu argued that allowing flexibility for deans lead to more efficient and effective resource utilization than general retention efforts offered.

Research relevant to the present study includes the factors that motivated longevity for higher education faculty (Marston & Brunetti, 2009). Marston and Brunetti (2009) examined job satisfaction of experienced and tenured professors at a mid-sized liberal arts college. For the purpose of the study, Marston and Brunetti gave the *experienced professors* label to tenure track faculty who had been teaching in academia for a minimum of 15 years. A total of 74 professors responded to the survey, and Marston and Brunetti subsequently interviewed 25 professors for in-depth responses. The participants in Marston and Brunetti's study represented the institution's four schools: Liberal Arts, Science, Education, and Economics and Business Administration. Marston and Brunetti noted that regardless of the institution's classification as comprehensive, the campus with about 2,600 students had the "look and feel" of an undergraduate liberal arts college (p. 325). Marston and Brunetti gave the faculty members the Experienced Teacher Survey (ETS), on which the respondents rate the importance of various factors that influence faculty life.

Several prominent intrinsic factors affect job satisfaction for higher education faculty. Interacting with students and helping them learn and grow was the overarching source of satisfaction for the professors as well as motivation to maintain an academic career (Marston & Brunetti, 2009). In fact, a love of learning was evident; the professors enjoyed their subjects and felt they were continually learning (Marston & Brunetti, 2009). Scholarship was an immensely valuable aspect of the professors' careers, which is not surprising given their compelling interest in their academic fields (Marston & Brunetti, 2009). Marston and Brunetti found that professional autonomy in the classroom was a significant source of satisfaction, suggesting that they might have sought a different position had there been policies that impinged on their freedom and flexibility. Extrinsic factors such as tenure or job security, compensation and benefits, and a flexible teaching schedule were also sources of satisfaction and

motivation to remain at the university, but these had less
of an impact than professional satisfaction (Marston &
Brunetti, 2009). For respondents in the Marston and
Brunetti study, lack of recognition for work well
accomplished was a persistent source of dissatisfaction
beyond the actual workload. Similarly, Safi, Khoshknab,
Russell, and Rahgozar (2011) sought to identify factors
leading to job satisfaction using a descriptive cross-
sectional study of 94 faculty members. In a principal
component analysis, the motivational domain had the
most impact while the economic domain had the least
impact on job satisfaction (Safi et al., 2011).

Relationships play a key role in motivating
longevity for higher education faculty (Marston &
Brunetti, 2009). Marston and Brunetti (2009) also found
professors'' relationships with colleagues played a
pivotal role in decisions to stay with the institution than
their relationships with administrators (Marston &
Brunetti, 2009). The importance the professors awarded
their collegial relationships also had a negative side; as
one professor acknowledged, "it's painful when it is not
there" (p. 330). The lack of support this respondent felt
from colleagues motivated the professor to cultivate
relationships with faculty in other departments (Marston

& Brunetti, 2009). Ultimately the college members elected her to a committee, and she found her career immensely rewarding (Marston & Brunetti, 2009). Other faculty members expressed frustration or dissatisfaction if they experienced similar lack of support (Marston & Brunetti, 2009). The qualitative responses in Marston and Brunetti's study were valuable for illuminating the various individual responses that arose due to similar institutional conditions. Fuller et al.'s (2008) assertion supports the idea that college administrators should develop collaborative ties as well as support and implement mentoring objectives for all faculty members.

Perhaps as a positive aspect, the professors interviewed for Marston and Brunetti's (2009) study invested more importance in their collegial relationships than their interactions with administrators. Interviews elicited a number of negative opinions about the administrators (Marston & Brunetti, 2009). One professor in the Marston and Brunetti study admitted that he had contemplated leaving on more than one occasion and that the issue of concern "was administratively induced" (p. 331). Interestingly, only 50% to 60% of leaders admit to being effective in the critical leadership skills needed to foster quality relations with employees

(Newhall, 2012). In studies by Bass and Riggio (2006), Bennis (2010), and Kouzes and Posner (2007) professors have described the qualities of an ideal administrator. These included the following: sharing common goals with faculty, actively listening and paying attention to faculty members' concerns, being supportive, displaying honesty and integrity, willing to work together with faculty to deal with challenges and solve problems, and being accessible and approachable. Broadly, the professors described the characteristics of an effective transformational leader; however, the administrators they encountered did not necessarily possess those attributes (Bass & Riggio, 2006; Bennis, 2010; Kouzes & Posner, 2007).

Several voluntary duties emerged as key factors that demotivated longevity for higher education faculty (Marston & Brunetti, 2009). Professors in the Marston and Brunetti (2009) study showed little enthusiasm for providing service to the institution. A common concern by faculty members, found by Marston and Brunetti, was that the demands for service were not fair and equitable. One professor felt it was 'servitude' rather than service and described the system as 'hierarchical' (Marston & Brunetti, 2009, p. 335). Professors reported their sense of expectation they would provide uncompensated service had the following effects: (a) detracted from the time and energy the professors desired to devote to their discipline and (b) seemed exploitive (Marston & Brunetti, 2009). Service was the only factor the professors considered less relevant to their job satisfaction and motivation to stay than the administration (Marston & Brunetti, 2009). Indeed, as described by Marston and Brunetti, a common attitude toward the administrators was "Let them do their thing and leave me alone" (p. 338). Faculty members in the Marston and Brunetti study listed the following as areas in which the administrators needed improvement to enhance the job satisfaction of their senior faculty: working to build better relationships with faculty, paying attention to faculty concerns, and learning better ways to resolve conflicts.

High workload can negatively affect faculty morale. Houston et al. (2006) focused on workload in their study of job satisfaction among faculty members in New Zealand. The large public university spans several campuses and has a sizable distance education program (Houston et al., 2006). Amidst major changes to the university system, workload policy emerged as a point of contention among increasingly pressured faculty members (Houston et al., 2006). The dataset used for analysis in Houston's et al. study sample came from three sources and covered 3 years. The Work Environment Survey (WES), first conducted in 2002, covered research on work stress and job satisfaction in universities in the United States, Canada, and Australia (Houston et al., 2006). The findings showed that it was not the increasing demands per se that were inducing negative feelings but rather the perception that administrators failed to recognize the faculty members for exemplary performance or supported in change efforts (Houston et al., 2006). There was some disagreement on whether morale was high or low. Respondents in the Houston study displayed high satisfaction regarding certain aspects, which included the following: professional autonomy, the degree of responsibility, and the extent of variety in their work. An excessive workload detracts from the teaching and research that attract individuals to academia (Houston et al., 2006).

The mixed feelings expressed by the New Zealand faculty members in the Marston and Brunetti (2009) study appear commonly in the literature. In interviews, however, Houston et al. (2006) noted the lack of creative problem solving in response to questions of how faculty members might themselves resolve the workload issues. Focus groups in Houston's et al. study revealed, in some respects, the university had adopted a culture of blame as opposed to proactive problem solving. Transformational leadership ideally meets the needs of challenging and uncertain conditions (Bass & Riggio, 2006), which may forestall the development of such negative trends. In particular, leadership characterized by idealized influence and intellectual stimulation should be a positive antidote to the passive culture expressed by the respondents in the Marston and Brunetti study.

Intrinsic and extrinsic rewards. Effective contingent reward (transactional leadership) had a positive impact on organizational commitment. O'Meara and Terosky (2008) conducted hundreds of in-depth interviews of faculty members. O'Meara and Terosky's analysis showed that environmental factors indirectly affected intentions to stay (through the environmental factors' effect on both job satisfaction and organizational commitment). O'Meara and Terosky noted that the external influence of job opportunity exerted a direct, negative impact on intentions to stay. Autonomy, communication, distributive justice, and role conflict had significant total effects on the intention to stay (O'Meara & Terosky, 2008). Autonomy operated indirectly through job satisfaction and organizational commitment, while faculty autonomy signifies trust on the part of the institution (O'Meara & Terosky, 2008). According to past research reviewed by O'Meara and Terosky, opportunities for faculty socialization, communication, and mentoring may enhance affective commitment. While salary can be a pivotal issue, especially in departments where salaries are low, the perception of fair compensation offers more value to job satisfaction than does a salary cutoff (O'Meara & Terosky, 2008).

Gender. Interest in gender as a characteristic affecting job satisfaction for higher education faculty has generated many findings. Reybold, Brazer, Schrum, and Corda (2012) studied knowledge and access as related to committee membership. Reybold et al. (2012) noted prior survey research by the Collaborative on Academic Careers in Higher Education included findings that, for women, factors of interest were tenure clarity and expectations, compensation and benefits, the nature of their teaching and research, balancing work and life, job climate and culture, and global satisfaction. Across disciplines, female faculty members expressed lower levels of job satisfaction in several areas when compared with male faculty members (Reybold et al., 2012). These areas were the number of hours worked, the amount of time for research, work/life balance, and the compatibility of the tenure track with raising children (Reybold et al., 2012). When Sabharwala and Corley (2009) explored faculty job satisfaction and retention for women, they too included several demographic, institutional, and career-related factors in their research model, yet they found that males were significantly less satisfied than females, when comparing overall job satisfaction. Seifert and Umbach (2008) explored the effects of demographic characteristics and discipline on job satisfaction using data from NSOPF:99. The framework for the study was Kalleberg's model of job satisfaction, which considers the interrelationships of individual characteristics and intrinsic and extrinsic rewards (Seifet & Umback, 2008). Female faculty members were significantly less satisfied with their professional autonomy than their male colleagues in the same discipline (Saifert & Umback, 2008). Adding further complexity to this picture, Akroyd, Bracken, and Chambers (2011) found that female college faculty members in general education disciplines expressed more satisfaction with their jobs than female faculty who taught in occupational areas. Women were also less satisfied with compensation and opportunities for advancement than men in the same discipline (Seifert & Umbach, 2008).

Ethnicity. Ethnicity affects job satisfaction for some higher education faculty. Seifert and Umbach (2008) found that ethnicity did not affect satisfaction with intrinsic rewards, in contrast to prior research reporting lower satisfaction among faculty of color. Akroyd et al. (2011) found that Caucasian men tended to be less satisfied than men of color. Faculty members with disabilities expressed lower satisfaction with intrinsic rewards (Akroyd et al., 2011). Asian faculty members and Latino faculty members also expressed less satisfaction with extrinsic rewards in the Akroyd et al. study. Akroyd et al. examined perceptions of equitable treatment. Akroyd et al. found that female and minority faculty members showed sensitivity to the presence of inequitable treatment for both female and minority faculty members. Likewise, Bozeman and Gaughan (2011) found that faculty members expressed dissatisfaction with their jobs when they perceived that the school did not pay according to their worth. Thus, as a summary, women tended to be less satisfied than men, and the tenured tended to be more satisfied than the untenured. In relation to the rationale for the presently proposed study, administration would be able to change any or all of the factors that influence differences in satisfaction and equitable treatment.

S.T.E.M. disciplines. Research comparing fields of study shows that aspects of a discipline affect job satisfaction for higher education faculty. Bozeman and Gaughan (2011) investigated the roles of individual characteristics, the work, and the institutional environment in job satisfaction using data from the 2004-2005 Survey of Academic Researchers, covering tenured and tenure-track faculty in science, technology, engineering, and mathematics (STEM). The sample in Bozeman and Gaughan's study consisted of 1,794 respondents. Slightly more women than men responded (Bozeman & Gaughan, 2011). The sources of job satisfaction fell into the three broad categories of

demographic characteristics, interactions with
colleagues, and extrinsic pay motivation (Bozeman &
Gaughan, 2011). Collegial relationships played a
powerful role in satisfaction; Bozeman and Gaughan
noted satisfaction was highly dependent upon the
respect that colleagues had for the professor and his or
her work. Bozeman and Gaughan noted respondent's
satisfaction with their pay was contingent on their
perception their pay was competitive on the job market.
Bozeman and Guaghan further noted gender had a
small, but significant impact, on job satisfaction. Of all
the variables in Bozeman and Gaughan's study, gender
had the weakest effect. Female faculty members
frequently feel subjected to a less welcoming climate
than their male colleagues, and past research widely
recognized the so-called chilly climate for women in the
STEM fields (Bilimoria, Joy, & Liang, 2008; Xu, 2008b).

Women in S.T.E.M. disciplines. Female higher
education faculty members express differences in job
satisfaction depending on their field of study. Settles et
al. (2006) focused on the organizational climate, which
women in the sciences experienced as not amenable to
their career progression. The participants in the Settles

et al. study were female tenure track faculty members in the natural sciences, engineering, and social sciences. Each respondent in the Settles et al. study held the rank of assistant professor, or a higher position, at a large Midwestern university. Settles et al. addressed experiences such as gender discrimination, sexist climate, positive climate, leadership, job satisfaction, productivity, and influence. The two features of organizational climate, sexist climate and gender discrimination, exerted the highest impact on overall job satisfaction (Settles et al., 2006). Gender discrimination also diminished the influence of women in their department (Settles et al., 2006). Settle's et al. noted supportive leadership led to higher job satisfaction. Settles et al. proposed women who experience a positive climate may more likely feel integrated into their department and less likely feel isolated.

Effective leadership by the department chair affected three positive work outcomes: influence, productivity, and job satisfaction (Bilimoria et al., 2008). Bilimoria et al. (2008) also noted leaders establish the organization's norms, values, and expectations for appropriate behavior. The findings in the study by Bilimoria et al.'s suggested clearly communicated expectations promote positive outcomes for female STEM faculty. This holds true even after controlling for gender discrimination and sexual harassment (Bilimoria et al., 2008). Bilimoria et al noted that women experienced the climate for women in the social sciences as much more favorable than in the life sciences and engineering. Nonetheless, Bilimoria et al. stated that the two groups were equivalent in job satisfaction, perceived influence, and productivity. Bilimoria et al. suggested that women in science may develop effective coping strategies that enable them to transcend a negative environment. However, female STEM faculty members still have high rates of attrition (Xu, 2008b).

Clinical and professional faculty. A study by Chung et al. (2010), investigated several characteristics affecting job satisfaction for higher education faculty members separated into academic and clinical groups. Chung et al. investigated the factors influencing the job satisfaction of academic faculty and clinical faculty at the University of Michigan Medical School. Although similar in many ways, their primary mission revolves around teaching and patient care without the research emphasis that defines tenure track academic faculty (Chung et al., 2010). There are notable structural differences between the two tracks. Chung et al. noted there had been no previous studies examining and comparing the job satisfaction of the two faculty groups. The sample included 353 academic track faculty members and 360 clinical track faculty members (Chung et al., 2010). There were some marked differences between the two groups (Chung et al., 2010). Men made up three-quarters of the instructional faculty but 57% of the clinical faculty, assistant professors comprised two-thirds of the clinical faculty, while full professors accounted for more than half the instructional faculty in Chung et al.'s study. Analysis of the participants' responses in the Chung et al. study produced the following factors that influence satisfaction: departmental leadership, autonomy, expectations, balance, basic science research, clinical support, teaching support, and compensation.

For both groups of faculty, the dominant influences on satisfaction related to autonomy, career expectations, work-life balance, and department leadership (Chung et al., 2010). The role of the department chair is critical in setting the culture of the

department (Chung et al., 2010). Chung et al. (2010)
also proposed that due to their experience, department
chairs may make excellent mentors for younger faculty
members. It is noteworthy that while mentorship per se
was not a significant factor in the satisfaction of either
faculty group, those respondents who had mentors
expressed significantly greater satisfaction than those
that did not (Chung et al., 2010). However, the clinical
faculty members in Chung et al.'s study were much less
satisfied with the quality of their mentoring relationships
and their opportunities for career advancement. Chung
et al. found department heads have the capacity to
establish formal channels for pairing mentors and
protégés. Team and group mentoring are also
alternatives to traditional mentorships and have the
advantage to exposing the protégés to mentors with
different styles and experiences (Chung et al., 2010).
Department chairs can also serve as informal mentors
through role modeling (Chung et al., 2010). Strategies
to enhance faculty job satisfaction more often affect the
outcome if undertaken at the department level with the
active involvement of the department chair (Chung et al.,
2010).

In a study of salary and promotion of clinical faculty, Froeschle and Sinkford (2009) explored dental faculty members' satisfaction and perceptions of their work environment. They conducted the research with 57 faculty members. Status and salary were pertinent issues as lower paid faculty members felt they had fewer resources and opportunities for professional development, including promotion and tenure workshops and mid-tenure review and feedback (Froeschle & Sinkford, 2010). Respondents in Froeschle and Sinkford's study who said they were not adequately mentored also stated (a) dissatisfaction with the available resources, (b) greater inclination to turn to external resources for development, and (c) lesser satisfaction with collegial relationships.

Another finding of the study showed faculty members who enjoyed positive mentorships with senior faculty reported much higher job satisfaction and a favorable work-life balance (Froeschle & Sinkford, 2010). Opportunities for professional growth, and above all strong mentoring relationships, appeared to be decisive factors in the dental faculty members' job satisfaction in Froeschle and Sinkford's study. For clinical faculty in Froeschle and Sinkford's (2009) study, women reported more intention to remain than did men. Faculty members in Froeschle and Sinkford's study placed importance on collegial relationships and assistance to students. The majority of respondents in Froeschle and Sinkford's study expressed intentions to remain in academia for the next 5 to 8 years; however, men were slightly more inclined than women to say they might leave. The two paramount reasons drawing them to remain in academia were similar to those of the veteran liberal arts faculty (Marston & Brunetti, 2009). In other words, relationships with their colleagues and students were main sources of satisfaction (Froeschle & Sinkford, 2009). For clinical faculty, positive relationships with colleagues and students may be pivotal to retaining them in academia. Hence, Froeschle and Sinkford state that institutions should enhance reward and recognition for teaching to retain dedicated dental faculty.

Leadership and support personnel also played a pivotal role in satisfaction (Froeschle & Sinkford, 2010). In the context of a faculty satisfaction survey, Froeschle and Sinkford viewed leadership as an elusive factor to quantify and measure. Froeschle and Sinkford noted many quantitative faculty surveys show evidence leadership influences faculty satisfaction without delving further into how this occurs. Surveys that inquire about faculty members' relationships with the department chair are an exception (Froeschle & Sinkford, 2010). Froeschle and Sinkford also noted influence of top leadership is indirect, and frequently must be inferred from conditions that either enhance or detract from satisfaction. Salary is often a point of dissatisfaction (Froeschle & Sinkford, 2010). For professional faculty who can earn higher incomes in the private sector, increasing intrinsic rewards and recognition may be pivotal to retaining them in the academic environment (Froeschle & Sinkford, 2009)

Pay exerts a primary influence on satisfaction of clinical faculty members. Pharmacy faculty members were the focus of research on satisfaction conducted by Spivey, Chisholm-Burns, Murphy, Rice, and Morelli (2009). Spivey et al. (2009) cited evidence there are escalating demands for pharmacy faculty, although many positions remain vacant.

Nursing programs have similar conditions (Baker, Fitzpatrick, & Griffin, 2011). Spivey et al. developed an online survey instrument for the study, and 266 pharmacy faculty members responded. The respondents in Spivey et al.'s study expressed (a) moderate levels of satisfaction with their jobs and fringe benefits and (b) moderate to high satisfaction with their opportunities to capitalize on their skills and abilities. Spivey et al.'s detailed analysis revealed that higher paid faculty members expressed more satisfaction with their work, compared to responses of lower paid faculty members. Demographic and institutional factors did not influence job satisfaction (Spivey et al., 2009). Spivey et al. attributed absence of gender differences in satisfaction, to the growing demand for pharmacy faculty and intensive efforts to eradicate gender inequality. The recommendations for increasing satisfaction and retention of pharmacy faculty apply to all disciplines (Spivey et al., 2009). Spivey et al.'s recommendations included the following:

- Actively promote a culture of awareness, equity, and appreciation for diversity;
- Develop equitable and transparent reward systems based on clear criteria;
- Create and sustain a work environment intellectually stimulating and challenging;

- Provide institutional support for scholarship and scholarly inquiry with adequate resources and opportunities for professional growth and development;

- Identify, create, promote, and disseminate opportunities for recognition and advancing knowledge;

- Devise strategies to promote a healthy work-life balance without compromising high standards;

- Seek opportunities to enhance the reputation of the department, program, and institution;

- Advocate on behalf of faculty for competitive salaries.

These recommendations can easily be matched to the four dimensions of transformational leadership and contingent rewards (Spivey et al., 2009).

Status and rank. The disparities in job satisfaction between senior, middle, and junior faculty found in the CAPS (Coates et al., 2010) warrants additional study. Rogotzke (2011) explored satisfaction related to rank. Rogotzke noted women were somewhat overrepresented. Satisfaction with the features of the university emerged as the overriding predictor of job satisfaction for tenure and tenure track faculty, a pattern that held for associate professors, assistant professors, and full professors (Rogotzke, 2011). Rogotzke found only instructors and academic professionals departed from that preference. Factors under this heading include support for collaboration, innovation and risk-taking, high quality work, high quality service, and a sense of community (Rogotzke, 2011).

Other research by Bozeman and Gaughan (2011) similarly investigated rank as a characteristic related to job satisfaction. Bozeman and Gaughan found that faculty members are more often satisfied with their jobs when they perceive their colleagues respect their research. Bozeman and Guaghan also found higher satisfaction among faculty when their compensation matches their estimation of what they are worth. Judgea, Piccolob, Podsakoffc, Shawd, and Riche (2010), in a meta-analysis not restricted to faculty members, estimated the population correlation between pay level and measures of pay and job satisfaction. As a result, pay level only marginally related to satisfaction. This is consistent with Rogotzke's (2011) finding that the level of pay was notable for all faculty members. In

Marston and Brunnetti's (2009) study, the significance of compensation decreased for assistant professors. Marston and Brunetti found that satisfaction with colleagues was significant for faculty of all ranks, consistent with the emphasis the veteran liberal arts faculty placed on their relationships with colleagues. Satisfaction with the department chair only maintained significance for assistant professors and academic professionals (Marston & Brunetti, 2009). Rogotzke attributed this to the fact assistant professors tend to be relative novices and thus might desire more attention and assistance from the department chair. This finding by Rogotzke (2011) explains why experienced liberal arts professors in the Marston and Brunetti study could dismiss their relationships with administrators as irrelevant to their satisfaction. Marston and Brunetti also noted work-family balance proves vital to some degree for all faculty ranks. In the final analysis for Marston and Brunetti, however, it was only significant for assistant professors and professors with conflict between work and family lives exerting a negative impact on satisfaction.

In this researcher's assessment of the findings, these studies regarding status and rank among faculty indicated gaining insight into the factors affecting the satisfaction of different faculty groups helps administrators address their concerns. Administrators may consider adapting support to individual needs and preferences as a primary example of individualized consideration.

From the perspective of person-to-job fit, Maynard and Joseph (2008) investigated the job satisfaction and commitment of college faculty in three categories: full-time faculty, part-time faculty who prefer a part-time position, and part-time faculty who would prefer a full-time position. Maynard and Joseph's study offer ample utility at a time when institutions of higher learning rely more extensively on adjunct faculty members than in the past. In fact, part-time faculty members constitute at least 40% of the faculty members in many institutions (Maynard & Joseph, 2008).

Maynard and Joseph (2008) also noted while some assume part-time faculty members feel less satisfied with their work, the empirical evidence does not support that belief. Maynard and Joseph argued the aggregated quantitative data may obscure crucial distinctions among part-time faculty. Thus, Maynard and Joseph's study distinguished between the two groups

they labeled voluntary and involuntary part-time faculty.
The full sample consisted of 167 respondents employed
at a comprehensive public university (Maynard &
Joseph, 2008). Maynard and Joseph used the
Minnesota Satisfaction Questionnaire (MSQ) to assess
job satisfaction. The Organizational Commitment
Questionnaire (OCQ) measured *affective* commitment
(Maynard & Joseph, 2008). The involuntary part-time
faculty members were theorized to be underemployed,
marked by over qualification and underpayment
(Maynard & Joseph, 2008).

The findings by Maynard and Joseph confirmed
involuntary part-time faculty members expressed more
dissatisfaction with compensation, opportunities for
advancement, and job security than the other two groups
expressed. All three groups in the Maynard and
Joseph's study expressed comparable satisfaction with
other facets of their work. Ironically, the part-time faculty
members, including the involuntary part-time faculty
members, expressed slightly stronger affective
commitment to the institution than did the full-time faculty
members (Maynard & Joseph, 2008). Maynard and
Joseph noted part-time faculty members expressed
more positive attitudes on several dimensions than full-

time faculty expressed.

Maynard and Joseph proposed institutions may be providing part-time faculty members with more support than many have recognized. An alternative explanation is the administration provided insufficient support to full-time faculty members, or faculty members may have higher expectations than the departments have prepared to meet (Maynard & Joseph, 2008).

If indeed part-time faculty members report greater attached to the institution and are at least as satisfied as their full-time colleagues, the trend toward hiring more part-time faculty members than full time members may have positive benefits for the institution. Maynard and Joseph (2008) suggested targeted recruitment aimed at hiring faculty members who prefer part-time positions. With impending retirements and a growing demand for faculty members who teach online courses, this may be an advantageous strategy for forward thinking administrators (Maynard & Joseph, 2008).

Community college faculty. Job characteristics of community college faculty differ somewhat from those of state colleges and universities. Shared governance is less prevalent at community colleges; many community colleges still adhere to a bureaucratic structure (Jenkins & Jensen, 2010). Community college faculty members have traditionally enjoyed much less professional autonomy than 4-year college faculty (Kim, Twombly, & Wolf-Wendel, 2008). Kim et al. (2008) noted unionization that prevails at community colleges also produces rules and policies that erode professional autonomy. Using data from the 2004 National Study of Postsecondary Faculty (NSOPF), Kim et al. (2008) explored the impact of professional autonomy on community college faculty member job satisfaction. They used a dataset that included personal and institutional characteristics.

The findings by Kim et al. (2008) showed most community college faculty members, regardless of their institutional type or faculty status and rank, expressed satisfaction with instructional autonomy. Undergraduate faculty members in doctoral and non-doctoral institutions in Kim et al.'s study expressed more satisfaction with instructional autonomy than community college faculty members expressed, while community college faculty members expressed higher overall satisfaction. The only effect for demographic factors was Asian and Latino/a faculty in 4-year institutions were less satisfied with instructional autonomy (Kim et al., 2008). Colleges and universities are at various stages in creating a positive diversity climate (Kezar, 2010). The quantitative NSOPF data does not shed light on why members of those ethic groups would be less satisfied with instructional autonomy and only at baccalaureate institutions (Kezar, 2010). Across institutional type and status, the same factors influenced satisfaction with autonomy (Kim et al., 2008).

Distance education faculty. Job characteristics for online courses differ somewhat from job characteristics of traditional courses. The demand for online courses is far outpacing the growth of any other sector of postsecondary education (Bolliger & Wasilik, 2009; Green et al., 2009). Bolliger et al. (2009) noted that the quality of distance education programs and courses is a serious issue to college officials. Bolliger et al. found that faculty members who have experience teaching online courses have more favorable opinions of online courses than those who have not. At the same time, as the demand for online courses escalates, so does the number of online faculty members (Bolliger, 2009). Retaining qualified online faculty should be a priority for institutions, which entails understanding the factors that influence the satisfaction of online faculty (Bolliger, 2009).

One profitable area of study addresses characteristics affecting job satisfaction for faculty members teaching online courses. Green et al. (2009) explored the factors affecting the involvement of online faculty in a study of 135 instructors from 23 universities, drawn from the listserv of the Distance Education Online Symposium as well as from current and former instructors of online courses at East Carolina University and California State University at Fullerton. The respondents in Green et al.'s study were fairly evenly divided among four groups: adjunct or part-time, full-time non-tenured, tenure track, and tenured. Green et al. noted slightly more than half the respondents taught online courses for 1-3 years, attesting to their relative novelty in the higher education landscape.

Online courses offer several benefits for faculty members. The main reasons for opting to teach distance courses included flexible working conditions, opportunity to use technology, opportunity to share knowledge with others, intellectual challenge, career development or advancement, and opportunity to acquire teaching experience (Green et al., 2009). Green et al. noted that the factors that would encourage the respondents to continue teaching online courses do not differ from those preferred by faculty who teach in person. These factors are as follows: continuous training provided by the institution, financial compensation that matched their workload, support from the institution, opportunities to assist with course or program development, and mentoring from experienced distance faculty (Green et al., 2009)

Faculty members differed in reasons for choosing to teach online courses. The tenured faculty diverged from the other three groups in that their predominant motivation to teach online courses is an intellectual challenge (Green et al., 2009). Explicitly and implicitly, intellectual challenge figured prominently in motivational factors of the veteran liberal arts faculty interviewed by Marston and Brunetti (2009). The tenured faculty also differed from other groups in that approximately one half cited the absence of a personal connection with the university as a discouragement from continuing to teach online courses (Green et al., 2009). Other distinctive differences, according to Green et al. (2009), were that loyalty to the institution as well as an opportunity for increased income motivated the adjunct and part-time faculty members. In contrast, the tenure track and untenured faculty appeared driven primarily by intrinsic rewards (Green et al., 2009). For the most part, Green et al. found the four groups were quite similar.

Administrators face several challenges in supporting faculty members teaching online courses. University leaders may never personally interact with some of their online faculty in a face-to-face setting (Green et al., 2009). They do play a powerful role in creating an environment conducive to their professional growth and commitment (Green et al., 2009). Based on findings, Green et al. made several recommendations. First, Green et al. (2009) emphasized that regardless of experience, online instructors desire continuous opportunities for professional growth and learning. Satisfying this interest also involves professional education and support, given that many online instructors lack technological expertise to format their course content as effective educational media (Green et al., 2009). Second, Green et al. suggested there should be a formal mentoring system for novice online instructors. Serving as mentors may also reinforce the commitment and enthusiasm of veteran online faculty

(Green et al., 2009). Third, Green et al. emphasized the importance of building a sense of community, particular for adjunct faculty who may teach online distance courses. Ongoing open communication is critical to that endeavor, noted Green et al. A leader's behavior associated with individualized consideration and intellectual stimulation may be pivotal to the satisfaction and commitment of online faculty (Green et al., 2009).

Faculty satisfaction as related to online courses also benefited from several qualitative study methods. Bolliger and Wasilik (2009) examined satisfaction among 122 instructors who taught distance courses at the University of Wyoming during Fall 2007 or Spring 2008. The university in Bolliger and Wasilik's (2009) study had been a pioneer in distance learning, having begun their distance education program in 1984. The school integrated the Online Faculty Satisfaction Survey (OFSS) into the university's course management system (Bolliger & Wasilik, 2009). The OFSS used in Bolliger and Wasilik's study had 36 questions divided into the three subscales of *student-related issues, instructor-related issues,* and *institution-related issues.* The student-related issues emerged as the most important, which is consistent with the strong student orientation of the liberal arts faculty (Marston & Brunetti, 2009).

Instructor-related issues directly affected satisfaction, but

counted as less important than student-related issues

(Bolliger & Wasilik, 2009). Bolliger and Wasilik found

institution-related issues, which consisted of workload,

compensation, preparation, and course evaluation, were

the least important. Of these four, however, workload

had the highest mean scores (Bolliger & Wasilik, 2009).

Roughly 60% of the instructors said their workload was

heavier when they taught online courses than teaching

in-seat courses (Bolliger & Wasilik, 2009). Green et al.

(2009) found workload to be particularly pertinent for the

full-time non-tenured distance faculty.

In view of the nature of the distance education

program at the University of Wyoming, distance

educators may already have ample professional support.

Learning and professional development issues, which

were highly influential to satisfaction and motivation of

distance faculty surveyed by Green et al. (2009), were

less valuable to Bolliger and Wasilik's (2009)

respondents. Bolliger and Wasilik were testing the

psychometric properties of the OFSS; thus they did not

elaborate on the responses of the instructors, which

would have provided additional insight into how the

factors that affect their satisfaction play out.

In a study of faculty satisfaction focused on quality management of online courses, Bolliger and Wasilik (2009) approached the issue from the perspective of quality enhancement. In the context of higher education, quality enhancement refers to continuous quality improvement in the quest to fulfill the institution's stated mission (Bolliger & Wasilik, 2009). Analogous to total quality management (TQM) in the corporate sector, continuous quality improvement in higher learning involves ongoing, systematic evaluation (Bolliger & Wasilik, 2009). Bollinger and Wasilik noted one of the key features of TQM is strong organizational leadership. Quality enhancement initiatives often fail due to lack of leadership support (Bolliger & Wasilik, 2009). Bolliger and Wasilik's recommendations for administrators were quite consistent with those of Green et al. (2009). Three essential features are community, compensation, and fair treatment (Bolliger & Wasilik, 2009). Online communities can serve multiple purposes, from being an educational resource to fostering a sense of collegiality (Bolliger & Wasilik, 2009). Bolliger and Wasilik noted that faculty members often form their own online communities. However, institutional support for

the development of online professional communities
shows the school recognized and valued online
instructors for their contributions to the university
(Bolliger & Wasilik, 2009).

Leadership and Job Satisfaction

Of the many job characteristics that affect job
satisfaction for higher education faculty members,
leadership style holds much promise for studies aimed at
retention. Mardanov et al. (2008) stated leadership is
one of the factors that may have an impact on employee
job satisfaction. Wong and Heng, (2009) asserted that
intentions to leave were closely related to the quality of
social relationships between the employees (instructors)
and administrators.

Community college faculty. Community college
administrators face unique challenges in faculty
retention. Klein and Takeda-Tinker (2009) explored the
impact of leadership on the job satisfaction of community
college faculty. Klein and Takeda-Tinker noted the focus
of their study, the Wisconsin Technical College System
(WTCS) plays a prominent role in the state economy by

increasing the earning power and employability of students who might otherwise not have access to higher education. Klein and Takeda-Tinker noted that a compelling mission drives the system. Low satisfaction on the part of college faculty may undermine the fulfillment of that mission at considerable financial and human cost (Klein & Takeda-Tinker, 2009). In Klein and Takeda-Tinker's study, all 16 colleges within the WTCS have seen an upsurge in turnover, due primarily to retirements. Finding and keeping qualified candidates for faculty and leadership positions is a critical issue, especially as the colleges seek to improve quality of education for students (Klein & Takeda-Tinker, 2009). This is a challenge, as new faculty management members come from a smaller pool of qualified applicants, due to a smaller population in the workforce as those from the baby-boomer population retire (Campbell et al., 2010; Finch et al., 2010).

Leadership style of community college administrators remains a vital area of study. As the main point of their study, Klein and Takeda-Tinker (2009) considered whether a relationship existed between the satisfaction of full-time business faculty and the leadership behaviors of their direct supervisor (Klein &

Takeda-Tinker, 2009). The instruments selected for the study were Spector's (2011) Job Satisfaction Survey and Kouzes and Posner's (2007) LPI. Klein and Takeda-Tinker also examined the prospective influence of demographic characteristics on the faculty members' job satisfaction and its relationship to leadership practices. A total of 215 faculty members completed the survey conducted by Klein and Takeda-Tinker; the participants were 55% female and the majority (58%) held a master's degree. The gender composition and degree attainment are fairly representative for community college faculty (Klein & Takeda-Tinker, 2009).

The findings present a persuasive case for the association between faculty members' job satisfaction and the leadership of their direct supervisor (Klein & Takeda-Tinker, 2009). Klein and Takeda-Tinker (2009) observed a strong association between the faculty members' satisfaction with their supervision and the supervisors' use of the five practices. Specifically, the higher the level of satisfaction, the higher the ratings the respondents awarded their supervisors (Klein & Takeda-Tinker, 2009). Klein and Takeda-Tinker found distinct relationships between (a) satisfaction with contingent reward leadership, communication, and promotion, and

(b) the respondents' assessment of their supervisors' leadership practices. Klein and Takeda-Tinker also found satisfaction with institutional operations, colleagues, and the nature of the work added to the relationship between satisfaction and leadership. The only measures of job satisfaction that failed to show a significant link with leadership practices were pay and benefits, which are not up to the supervisor in the heavily unionized WTCS (Klein & Takeda-Tinker, 2009). There are few such studies at 4-year or 2-year colleges (Klein & Takeda-Tinker, 2009).

Professional nursing faculty. Study of the leadership style of nursing administrators offers findings possibly unique to this discipline. Chen et al. investigated the relationship between the job satisfaction of nursing faculty and the leadership styles of their deans or directors (as cited in Cummings et al., 2009). Chen et al. (as cited in Cummings et al., 2009) used the MLQ-5X to assess leadership and the MSQ to rate job satisfaction. Chen et al.'s study took place in Taiwan where educational institutions show dedication to improving the quality of nursing education. Chen et al. found that followers expressed less satisfaction "with the contingent reward dimension of transactional leaders and individualized consideration of transformational leaders" (as cited in Riaz & Haider, 2010, p. 30). Similarly, Jansen et al. "concluded that the transformational leadership behaviors contribute significantly to exploratory innovation, while transactional leadership behaviors facilitate improving and extending existing knowledge" (as cited in Riaz & Haider, 2010, pp. 30-31). Jansen et al. described transactional leadership as associated with exploitative innovation (as cited in Riaz & Haider, 2010). Ayman and Korabik (2010) pointed out while transformational leadership is almost universally practiced, the behaviors displayed by transformational leaders may differ according to culture.

Active and passive leadership styles correlate conversely with job satisfaction levels. Individualized consideration and contingent reward leadership, which strongly relate to each other, acted as the main contributors to the nursing faculty members' job satisfaction, while the passive nature of *management by exception* adversely affected job satisfaction (Chen et al., as cited in Cummings et al., 2009). These three types of leadership explained most of the variance in job satisfaction. (Chel et al., as cited in Cummings et al.,

2009). Management by exception is antithetical to individualized consideration (Bass & Riggio, 2006). The greater extent the directors relied on passive management by exception, the less satisfied the educators were with their jobs (Bass & Riggio, 2006). Cummings et al. (2009) found "leadership focused on task completion alone was not sufficient to achieve optimum outcomes for the nursing workforce" (p. 1). Leaders in smaller schools exercised transformational leadership to a greater extent than in larger schools (Cummings et al., 2009). Chen et al. suggested it may be easier to communicate a shared vision to a smaller group (as cited in Cummings et al., 2009). This pattern somewhat parallels the greater use of participative leadership that Sirkis (2011) describes as observed in leaders of smaller departments.

Contingent reward leadership surpassed individualized consideration in predicting job satisfaction. Chen et al. ascribed this effect to the hierarchical nature of Confucian culture, which would favor, transactional leadership (as cited in Bennis et al., 2009). A strong preference for a fair reward and incentive system is virtually universal among college faculty (Bennis et al., 2009). The strong, positive influence of contingent

reward and individualized consideration, as well as the
negative impact of passive leadership styles, transcends
cultural and national boundaries (Bennis et al., 2009).

Empowerment. Baker et al. (2011) used
Kanter's model of structural empowerment as a
framework for examining the job satisfaction of nursing
instructors in associate degree nursing programs.
According to Kanter's theory, access to information,
resources, support, and opportunities to learn and
develop are foremost among the empowering elements
that can have pronounced impact on employees'
confidence, job satisfaction, commitment, and
productivity. The participants were 176 faculty members
from associates degree (ADN) programs within the
California Community College System (as cited in Baker
et al., 2011). Overall, Kanter found nursing instructors
had a moderate degree of structural empowerment.
Kanter noted the highest scores were for the *opportunity*
subscale, indicating the instructor's work was
challenging, and they were able to acquire new
knowledge and skills and perform tasks that allowed
instructors to apply their knowledge and skills. At the
opposite end, Kanter noted, the lowest scores were on

resources, signifying instructors had insufficient time to carry out all their work. Psychological empowerment was also moderate, with the highest scores signifying that (a) instructor's work was personally meaningful and respected and (b) instructors felt confident and competent in performing their work, noted Kanter. Perceptions of autonomy, control, and influence were lower (Kanter, as cited in Baker et al., 2011)

The association between psychological empowerment and job satisfaction was relatively high (Kanter, as cited in Baker et al., 2011). When, faculty respondents derived a sense of meaning, competence, autonomy, and power from work, they expressed increased job satisfaction, noted Kanter. Empowering leaders ensures that their followers have access to structures that produce empowerment (Kanter, as cited in Baker et al., 2011). Castro, Perifian, and Bueno (2008) proposed positive impact of transformational leaders on job satisfaction and commitment might operate through the mechanism of psychological empowerment. Castro et al. noted psychological empowerment mediated the effects of transformational leaders on job satisfaction and affective commitment. Baker et al. (2011) used the empowerment frameworks

to examine job satisfaction in staff nurses. The
juxtaposition of psychological empowerment and
transformational leadership might be useful for exploring
job satisfaction and commitment in academic faculty,
especially given the powerful role of autonomy in the
satisfaction of academics (Baker et al., 2011). Personal
meaning in work was a paramount theme in the
comments of the professors interviewed by Marston and
Brunetti (2009).

Turnover Intentions

As noted in the previous chapters, many
characteristics affect job satisfaction. Over time, job
dissatisfaction leads to voluntary turnover (DeConinck,
2009). In higher education, many administrators
recognize turnover as a critical issue, because a 5%
increase in retention can lead to a 10% decrease in
costs (Wong & Heng, 2009). The following sub-sections
discuss topics related to turnover, including gender and
ethnicity and perceived fairness; discipline-specific
influences on turnover; as well as issues for research
universities and community colleges.

Gender and ethnicity. Gender and race figured prominently in studies exploring faculty member turnover intentions. Cropsey et al. (2008) explored reasons that women and minority faculty members chose to leave a school of medicine in a survey of 166 faculty members who left the school from July 2001 to 2005. Cropsey et al. found the three most prevalent reasons were related to career or professional advancement, low salary, and issues with department leadership. For women, noted Crospey et al., issues with department chairs headed the list. At the time they left, the women and minority men were at lower ranks and with lower salaries (Crospey et al., 2008). Crospey et al. noted women comprise roughly half the students entering medical school yet female faculty members still face an inhospitable climate. Department chairs seem to play a direct role in the attrition of female and minority faculty (Crospey et al., 2008). At the institutional level, leadership plays an indirect but powerful role in creating a positive diversity climate (Crospey et al., 2008).

Science, Technology, Engineering, and Math (S.T.E.M.) disciplines. As discussed previously, discipline-specific characteristics also affect turnover intentions. Xu (2008b) examined turnover intentions and attrition among female faculty members in STEM disciplines in order to gain better insight into the under-representation of women faculty members in those fields. Two proposed models are the *pipeline model* and the *deficit model*, which approach the issue from the perspectives, respectively, of (a) flow of women into the sciences from grade school through graduate school with 'leakages' reducing the numbers, and (b) the inhospitable climate and obstacles to advancement that cause women in the sciences to leave academia (Xu, 2008b). The deficit model aligns with the empirical evidence on faculty turnover and the status of women in the academy (Xu, 2008b). Xu used data from NSOPF 1999 because the 2004 survey eliminated questions related to intentions to leave.

One proposed explanation for the under-representation of female faculty in STEM disciplines relates to the unsupported pipeline model. Research fails to support the idea that women place family responsibilities over work commitment (Xu, 2008b). The data showed no support for that assumption (Xu, 2008b). Xu noted women and men reported comparable time constraints, work demands (including

anticipated demands), and work commitment. The
results also failed to support the idea that a 'leakage' in
the supply pipeline accounts for the under-
representation of women in STEM fields (Xu, 2008b).
Women do not intend to leave their faculty positions at a
higher rate than men; however, women enter STEM
faculty positions in much fewer numbers (Xu, 2008b).
Based on the analysis, the most plausible explanation is
women experience negative work experiences leading to
higher rates of turnover, despite women and men initially
having equivalent levels of commitment and intentions to
stay (Xu, 2008b). The findings of Bilimoria et al. (2008)
supported that conclusion. Women who enter STEM
faculty positions seek supportive leadership, equal
access to resources, and equal opportunities for
advancement and promotions, but their expectations are
often not met (Xu, 2008b). Note that the female
pharmacy faculty desire the same conditions and show
less likelihood of facing structural obstacles in attaining
them (Spivey et al., 2009). On the other hand, female
medical faculty members encounter obstacles that
contribute to turnover (Cropsey et al., 2008). Thus, the
recommendations of Spivey et al. (2009) for creating an
equitable and positive work climate to attract and retain

talented and committed pharmacy faculty members prove even more crucial for STEM departments than other departments.

Many faculty members have stated academic institutions need to improve faculty diversity and provide greater career advancement opportunities for under-represented groups. For example, Apostolou, Hassell, Rebele, and Watson (2010) found this result when they reviewed studies of accounting faculty regarding diversity issues and the academic environment. Apostolou et al. found that higher proportions of women and minority faculty felt diversity issues merited attention and support. Apostolou et al. found a majority of women and minorities stated professional and academic organizations need to improve faculty diversity. About one-third of the respondents said diversity initiatives at their institution were ineffective (Apostolou et al., 2010).

There were definite inequities based on gender. Women accounting faculty had lower salaries and terminal degrees, less seniority, were less likely to have tenure, and were less visible in the ranks of associate and full professors (Apostolou et al., 2010). Despite the reported satisfaction with their present status by about three-quarters of the respondents, the written comments

of women and the minority faculty members disclosed
perceived discrimination (Apostolou et al., 2010). A
slight majority of minority faculty members felt they faced
barriers to advancement due to ethnic discrimination
(Apostolou et al., 2010). As a consequence, Apostolou
et al. noted women and minorities showed more
tendencies to express intentions to leave their present
institution, and this predilection showed as more
prevalent among minorities than women. It is up to the
college president to exercise leadership to promote
effective diversity policies and initiatives (Kezar, 2010).

Discipline-specific focus offers an avenue for
addressing female attrition from STEM faculty. Xu
(2008a) argued for the importance of recognizing
discipline-specific factors that influenced faculty
turnover. Using the NSOPF:99 data, Xu identified
several key factors linked with turnover and analyzed the
data to investigate the extent to which these factors were
stable or varied across different disciplines. Xu
organized the various disciplines into clusters, and the
analyses revealed patterns in each of the clusters that
can be used to target efforts effectively to reduce faculty
turnover. Xu noted that one recommendation for the
HPL (hard/pure/life) science cluster makes the climate

more hospitable to women and minorities, particularly Asians. The distinctions lay not so much in the factors that contribute to turnover and job satisfaction (which are similar across disciplines), but in prioritizing what is most desired by faculty in that department (Xu, 2008b). For example, one department might emphasize increasing autonomy in teaching and research, while another would be improved with an increase in supportive leadership, and another department warrants more equitable opportunities for advancement (Xu, 2008a). The discipline-specific approach is potentially highly valuable given the high costs of turnover (Xu, 2008a).

A workforce shortage and a faculty shortage in the pharmaceutical field intensify the need to reduce turnover. Taylor and Berry (2008) examined turnover intentions among pharmacy faculty. There are already vacancies that remain unfilled (Spivey et al., 2009). Taylor and Berry noted earlier research found the main reasons for considering leaving were excessive workload, desire for new challenges, low salary, and negative relationships with colleagues and administrators. Roughly 20% of the respondents considered leaving their institution (Taylor & Berry, 2008). Taylor and Berry suggested support from the department chair and institutional leadership are essential for promoting commitment to the institution, thus essential for decreasing turnover intensions. The leaders have power to create conditions to facilitate satisfaction and commitment (Taylor & Berry, 2008).

Research universities. Stress factors and dissatisfaction with conditions heighten the likelihood that faculty members' will consider leaving academia, while positive fit and support decreased the likelihood of leaving. Polio, Krupat, Civian, Ash, and Brennan (2012) investigated intentions to leave among faculty members at a large public research university. Polio et al. analyzed responses from a sample of tenured or tenure track faculty members. Polio et al. noted the findings support Xu's (2008a) assertion that factors driving turnover differ according to disciplines. In heavily research-oriented disciplines, Xu concluded cutting down on committee work and faculty meetings would help reduce turnover. Excessive workload increases turnover intentions (Houston et al., 2006). These factors, along with teaching underprepared students, were all stress factors contributing to turnover intentions (Polio et al., 2012). Polio et al. noted that, higher productivity predicted intentions to leave, presumably for a more prestigious institution.

The findings indicated areas where administration can improve conditions for research opportunities to decrease turnover intentions. None of the factors related to fit, support, and satisfaction significantly correlated with considering the prospect of leaving for another institution (Polio et al., 2012). Family responsibilities and dissatisfaction with conditions – such as compensation, autonomy, workload, opportunities for advancement, and opportunities to pursue research – all heightened the probability of contemplating leaving academia (Polio et al., 2012). Alternatively, positive fit and support decreased the prospect of leaving academia (Polio et al., 2012).

Community colleges. Members of campus administration could increase faculty job satisfaction through improving elements under their control. Using structural equation modeling, Rosser and Townsend (2006) tested a model for understanding the factors underlying turnover intentions among community college faculty using data from NSOPF:99. Rosser and Townsend selected the variables in their model

specifically to capture the work environment at public 2-
year colleges. Aspects of faculty work life included
administrative support and facilities, professional
development, and technology support (Rosser &
Townsend, 2006). Job satisfaction included the intrinsic
factors of faculty decision-making authority, student
advising, course preparation, and workload, plus the
extrinsic rewards of salary, benefits, and job security
(Rosser & Townsend, 2006).

Among demographic factors, age related to
satisfaction and intentions to leave. Older faculty
members were more satisfied with their work and less
inclined to leave (Rosser & Townsend, 2006). Those
who had been at the institution longer were less satisfied
with their work (Rosser & Townsend, 2006). Rosser and
Townsend noted quality of the faculty's work life at the
institution appears to be foremost in their job
satisfaction. Rosser and Townsend discovered of the
three components of faculty work life, administrative
support and facilities emerged as the most important.
Rosser and Townsend noted budget cuts are resulting in
smaller secretarial staffs, limited funding for libraries,
and larger class sizes, thereby creating antithetical
conditions to what faculty members desire at 2-year and

4-year institutions. Rosser and Townsend surmised these changes might play a role in the lower satisfaction of long term faculty members, especially for members previously accustomed to more favorable conditions than offered currently. Unwelcome changes appeared to account for the low satisfaction of faculty members in Australia and the U.K. (Coates et al., 2010).

Several effects of transformational leadership appear in research regarding community college administration. Transformational leaders effectively secure employees' commitment to organizational change under conditions in which the changes have a direct and dramatic impact on their work (Herold, Fedor, Caldwell, & Liu, 2008). According to Herold et al. (2008), inspiration through vision, empowerment through active involvement, and sensitivity to followers' needs, combined with a commitment to justice and fairness, may help employees get through a change initiative. The researchers credited the relational aspect of transformational leadership with providing extra support amidst rampant change (Herold et al., 2008)

Community college faculty responded differently from findings for state and university faculty in a quality of work life survey. Technical support was a key factor in quality of faculty work life, which Rosser and Townsend (2006) attributed to a widespread integration of technology into the daily life of faculty. Professional development appeared less significant when compared to technical support in the same study (Rosser & Townsend, 2006). Rosser and Townsend suggested the definition of professional development might have been less relevant to community college faculty. Rosser and Townsend found all three facets of faculty work life had a positive impact on the faculty members. Rosser and Townsend did note the impact of benefits and security was negligible. Rosser and Townsend stated this was probably due to the prevalence of unionization (>70% of the study's faculty members held union membership). For unionized employees, salary and benefits are largely beyond the control of college administrators (Rosser & Townsend, 2006). Advising, course preparation, and workload were not highly pertinent, nor were decision-making authority and instructional autonomy (Rosser & Townsend, 2006). Community college faculty members have traditionally had less influence on decision making, and most faculty members express satisfaction with their instructional autonomy (Kim et al., 2008). Rosser and Townsend (2006) concluded community college faculty members are essentially satisfied with those aspects of work life they examined. Rosser and Townsend emphasized community college leaders need to honor the commitment of faculty members who show dedication to teaching at their institution.

Transition and Summary

There is an ample body of research on faculty job satisfaction, but relatively few studies that focus on the relationship between job satisfaction and academic leadership. This is a significant gap given that faculty members' relationships to the department chair can have a powerful impact on their satisfaction and turnover intentions (Bilimoria et al., 2008; Xu, 2008a). The department chair sets the tone for the department (Chung et al., 2010). The leadership of the chair can be a pivotal factor in the experience of women and minority faculty, who often perceive an inequitable and inhospitable climate (Chung et al., 2010). Some veteran faculty members reported their relationships with administrators have negligible effects on their job satisfaction (Marston & Brunetti, 2009). However, Marston and Brunetti (2009) noted their comments revealed they simply ignore administrators they feel are ineffective leaders. Department chairs likely have a much stronger effect on new faculty members who need support and mentoring, and the role model for new faculty members (Marston & Brunetti, 2009).

In summary, executive leaders play an indirect but immensely powerful role in faculty job satisfaction. Most of the factors that influence faculty job satisfaction and turnover intentions are under the control of the administration. Organizational culture and climate influence factors such as fair and competitive compensation, opportunities for advancement and promotion, professional autonomy, recognition for exemplary performance, support for teaching and research, and equitable treatment. Executive management largely controls the culture and climate and thus arguably controls these factors. In terms of leader behaviors, the synthesis of transformational (individualized consideration) and transactional (contingent reward) styles closely aligns with the preferences and concerns of faculty members. These behaviors can exert a powerful impact on faculty satisfaction and commitment when exercised by administrators at the department and upper levels.

CHAPTER 2
The Project

In colleges and universities, faculty achievers often move into leadership positions without the necessary training or knowledge about the role expectations for such positions (Klein & Takeda-Tinker, 2009). This lack can cause difficulties in establishing quality relations with other faculty members (Klein & Takeda-Tinker, 2009), possibly other administrators, and even the community. Only 50% to 60% of leaders admit to being effective in the critical leadership skills needed to foster quality relations with employees (Newhall, 2012). Creating awareness of effective leadership models for academic leaders may provide economic benefits to universities in the form of higher retention rates and greater commitment to the university. Through the present study, I attempted to increase awareness of effective leadership models for academic leaders. This chapter provides a detailed description of this study's method and procedures.

Purpose Statement

Efforts to curb costly faculty turnover should focus on employee job satisfaction characteristics. Supervisory leadership is one of the factors that may have an impact on employee job satisfaction (Mardanov et al., 2008). This potential impact largely accounts for the greater amount of attention focused on importance of various leadership models. If better assessments can be made of the relationship between these factors and overall employee satisfaction, it may be possible to align leadership strategies with greater organizational effectiveness and efficiencies. The purpose of this quantitative study was to determine the relationship, if any, between how faculty members evaluate academic administrator leadership styles and their personal job satisfaction within an institution in the State University System of Florida.

Role of the Researcher

The researcher had an affiliation with the Florida State College System, but no affiliation nor relationship with the State University System of Florida. Therefore, the researcher had no affiliation with the subject university in this study. The researcher administered the online surveys and also collected data in a valid and reliable manner by monitoring response rates. The researcher verified the sample of respondents accurately represented the target population's demographics. For the current study, the researcher used job satisfaction (JSS) and leadership instruments (MLQ). Current researchers justifiably have confidence in valid results if they follow the accepted and proper use of these tools (Gill, Mand, Culpepper, Mathur, & Bhutani, 2011). Other researchers (Bass & Avolio, 2012; Batayneh & Mohammad, 2011; Darshan & Shibru, 2011) have previously demonstrated that certain components of the MLQ can be reliably tied to job satisfaction as well as perceived leadership. For the present study, the researcher intended to maximize the validity of the findings in accordance with performance and ethical expectations relating to faculty members. Klein and Tinker (2009) and several other researchers have raised the issue of how faculty members view job performance differently, and the present study built on prior findings.

Participants

The participants selected for this study were full-time faculty members within an institution in the State University System of Florida. They included full professors, associate professors, assistant professors, instructors, and lecturers. First, the researcher completed the Walden University Institutional Review Board (IRB) application. Then, upon receiving conditional approval by Walden University, the researcher sought IRB approval through the subject university. Finally, the researcher submitted the subject university's approval to Walden for final approval consideration. The subject university had agreed to review the IRB application submitted to Walden University to ensure the application contained all the information required for the subject university's IRB approval, which eliminated unnecessary returns. The subject university agreed to provide a database of all full-time faculty email addresses upon both university approvals to the researcher. In the State of Florida, faculty email addresses are public information.

All full-time faculty members who teach within an institution in the State University System of Florida comprised the overall population for this study. A large sample size offers greater statistical strength and validity than a small sample size (Muenjohn & Armstrong, 2008). A large sample size was manageable because (a) the data collection procedures involved a self-administered survey and (b) the survey software allowed for ease of data management. The data analysis software sorted the data electronically. Self-selection determined inclusion or exclusion.

The researcher created the survey questions and used the online Survey Monkey polling platform for delivery of the survey after the receipt of the IRB approval from both Walden University and the subject university. The software generated a web link the researcher emailed to all faculty members in the email dataset. The email message consisted of a recruitment message and a link to the online website where the consent form and survey displayed. When a respondent clicked on the web link, the online consent form appeared. Participants read and accepted the terms of the consent form by clicking an acceptance button and then proceeded to the survey. There was no time limit on how long a participant chose to read the informed consent page. The survey remained open for completion for 4 weeks. The consent page consisted of the principal investigator's contact information and allowed for the opportunity to submit questions before beginning. Since participants implied consent by proceeding past the first page of the website, participant data were anonymous. Subjects participated from any computer and at the time of their choosing. This made it possible to participate in a private setting and at a time that did not bring attention to participation. Username and password credentials unique to the survey administrator protected the online survey platform. The researcher did not track IP addresses of respondents, which ensured anonymity for the respondents. As stated further in this chapter, the researcher did not collect or store identifying information. Upon downloading the de-identified raw data for analysis in SPSS, the researcher stored the data on an external hard drive to be kept in a passcode locked and safe location for a period of 5 years as required by Walden University's IRB at the time of human subject approval.

Research Method and Design

Three types of methodologies are available to researchers when conducting studies. These methodologies are quantitative, qualitative, and mixed methods (Muenjohn & Armstrong, 2008). The researcher gave consideration to all three methodologies during the process of choosing a research method for this project. Because the intent was to capture the beliefs and job satisfaction of a large number of faculty members, a quantitative approach was the most appropriate. Belli (2008) described a classification of research design based on purpose, which can be descriptive, predictive, or explanatory. The present study qualified as predictive, because the main usefulness of this study would be in a predictive capacity (Belli, 2008). While this limited the amount of detailed information that could be captured for any one respondent, it had the advantage of being more generalized to a larger population of faculty members in this or other Florida universities.

Method

Researchers using quantitative methods collect data from respondents and apply statistical methods to uncover patterns in the data (Schweitzer, 2009). Qualitative research, on the other hand, eschews numbers in favor of collecting detailed, descriptive information from a much smaller number of observational units (Symonds & Gorard, 2010). Additionally, Symonds and Gorard (2010) described a third method that uses various elements of quantitative and qualitative methods as the mixed methods approach to research. The researcher initially considered each of these three methods when choosing a method for this study. For reasons described in this chapter, the quantitative research method appeared the best suited.

The present study qualifies as positivist in approach. Henderson (2011) described positivists as researchers who use quantitative methods to predict the relationships between variables and use observations to test predictions derived from theory. As the researcher intended to examine the relationship between leadership styles and job satisfaction and to collect and analyze numerical data (Schweitzer, 2009), the quantitative research method was most appropriate for this study.

Research Design

The study design was correlational, with the
model providing a prediction as to which variables
moved up and down in parallel with the odds of
satisfaction. The researcher used logistic regression as
the statistical design. Logistic regression uses a model
of job satisfaction while considering control variables.
The prediction resulting from a logistic regression model
is either a probability or the odds of a faculty member
being satisfied with his or her job. The goal of prediction
is to get a significant estimate of what the value of the
dependent variable will be on the basis of known
independent variable values (Kawada & Yoshimura,
2012).

The results of this study relied on observational
data at a point in time rather than data collected in a
controlled setting (Henderson, 2011; Schweitzer, 2009).
Thus, I chose a multivariate method for statistical
analysis that controlled for possible confounding
variables (Siemsen & Roth, 2010). This method allowed
for the use of transformational, transactional, and
passive avoidant leadership styles in the same model
while controlling for possible effects of the demographic

variables. The researcher chose the correlational design because the study did not need to include manipulation, treatment, or modification of environment or participants to meet the research objectives (Belli, 2008). Participants were not randomly assigned to a group or given a treatment; hence, nonexperimental design aligned with the objectives of the study (Belli, 2008). A correlational study limits the ability to assert causation (Kawada & Yoshimura, 2012). While experiments may do a better job at demonstrating a causal relationship, it is not feasible to develop an experiment that randomly assigns faculty members to experience different leadership styles. Among all of the different possible research designs, the correlational design was the best design for understanding the relationship between leadership styles and job satisfaction.

Population and Sampling

The study sample was composed of the entire population of full-time faculty members who taught at a single institution in the State University System of Florida. The university had 567 full-time faculty members. The researcher expected a response rate of

18%. Given the current state of the literature on online survey response rates; this was a decidedly conservative number (Miller & Dillman, 2011). The results of a recent survey study indicated response rates were in the 42% to 59% range (Miller & Dillman, 2011). The proper selection of a population and sample size is critical to the success of a research project (Henderson, 2011). The purpose of sample size determination is to make it possible a population representative of a target population and is large enough to minimize the effects of random variation (Henderson, 2011). A response rate of 18% would yield a sample of 102. A power analysis, as discussed below, revealed this response rate to yield a sufficient sample size to find a medium effect size to be significant. A 40% response rate, closer to findings from the studies cited above, would have yielded a sample of 226, which is sufficient to uncover a small effect size (Fowler, 2008). The researcher worked with the chosen university's faculty research sponsor to identify the optimal time for survey distribution. Survey respondents had four weeks to participate in the survey and the researcher sent a reminder email after the first week and a final reminder before the last week.

The number of completed surveys returned resulted in an adequately large sample size, which met the criterion for adequate statistical power for the planned analyses. *Statistical power* refers to the probability of rejecting a null hypothesis when it is, in fact, false (Faul, Erdfelder, Buchner, & Lang, 2009). Because standard errors – and hence confidence intervals – are determined in part by sample size, a power analysis can determine the number of subjects needed to yield a significant result. The researcher relied primarily on logistic regression and thus used a power analysis to determine the necessary sample size for identifying a small, medium, or large logistic regression coefficient. The power analysis relied on the powerlog program written for Stata (Faul, Erdfelder, Buchner, & Lang, 2009). The power analysis used the effect size values of .1, .2, and .3 for large, medium, and small, respectively. Effect size values for this logistic regression referred to changes in predicted probability of observing faculty member satisfaction. Because the rate of change varies in logistic regression depending on where an observation falls along the logistic curve, these values reflected a change around .5 (the center of the curve). Unlike the effect sizes described by Faul et al.

(2009), there are not well-established conventions for determining what constitutes a small versus large effect size for logistic regression.

The researcher evaluated a sample size required for each of three effect sizes to achieve a power of .8 (i.e., an 80% probability of correctly rejecting the null hypothesis of no relationship) with a .05 cut-off for significance level. For the largest-effect size, the required sample size is 81. For a medium-effect size, the required sample size is 98. The required number of subjects is 219 to observe the smallest-effect size. In this study, 104 participants completed the survey, which was sufficient for a medium effect size.

There was no pilot data from the target population to determine which effect size to expect. Because of the online administration of the survey, costs of adding respondents were minimal. There were 567 full-time faculty members who received an invitation to participate in the survey. With a participation rate of 18.3%, the sample size was sufficient to detect a moderate effect size.

Given that previous research had found the MLQ to relate to job satisfaction (Rowold & Schlotz, 2009), the researcher expected a minimum effect size of 0.1, where as previously discussed, effect size is the change in predicted probability.

Ethical Research

The researcher invited full-time faculty at a state university to participate in this study. Participants received a link to the online survey, which began with a consent form. he researcher provided a description of the purpose of the study, the selection process for the participants, sample questions from the survey, the voluntary nature of the study, risks and benefits to being in the study, incentives, the privacy policy, IRB contact information, and my contact information.

Each participant gave implied consent to the terms described in the consent form by clicking the link at the end of the online consent form to proceed to the survey. The informed consent form stated that (a) each participant, at any time during the survey, may decide not to continue, and (b) this decision will have no consequence for the participant.

The researcher did not collect IP addresses, thus indirect identification on the basis of combining demographic data was nearly impossible, given that little demographic information was collected. The researcher included only three demographic variables in the survey: gender, tenure status, and ethnicity and each of these were coded as variables dichotomously, ensuring the anonymity of each subject's characteristics.

The informed consent also summarized the risks to the subject, which were minimal. The identified risks were the possibility of experiencing stress or fatigue, or of becoming upset. There were no anticipated economic or physical risks. There was no incentive or compensation for completing the study; however, individual participants might benefit to the extent that study findings may contribute to social change by creating awareness of effective leadership models and job satisfaction in Florida universities. These benefits outweighed risks involved in participating in the survey, which were no more than experienced in daily life, and they accrued to all faculty members equally. To minimize the risks, subjects who experienced these symptoms could drop out of the survey at any time. It was not likely the symptoms would be severe enough to require follow-up care. There was no explicit or implicit coercion involved in the data collection. All participation was voluntary, and there were no consequences for not participating. The researcher did not have any relationship with the subjects and, therefore, was not in any position of authority over them. The sample participants included university faculty with no further exclusion criteria applied. Being highly educated and familiar with the ethics of research, this is a group that is not typically considered vulnerable. It was possible some subjects would have a disability, but screening for this information would be overly invasive given the scope of the research questions.

The researcher kept raw data secure on a password-protected external drive and will keep records of raw data for a period of at least five years as required by Walden University. No person accessed identifiable raw data, as the researcher did not collect identifying information.

Data Collection

Instruments

The study made use of three survey instruments. This included the Multifactor Leadership Questionnaire (MLQ) Form 5x-Short, Spector's Job Satisfaction

Survey, and a brief demographic survey.

The MLQ-5x is a 45-item questionnaire that takes into consideration seven areas when assessing a leader's behavior (Bass & Avolio, 2012). These areas are intellectual stimulation, individualized consideration, contingent reward, and laissez-faire behaviors. According to the operational definition for the present study, a leader displays transformational leadership behaviors when he or she scores highly with regards to individualized consideration and motivation factors (Bass & Avolio, 2012). A five-point frequency rating scale uses the following numerical scale: 0 = *not at all*, 1 = *once in a while*, 2 = *sometimes*, 3 = *fairly often*, and 4 = *frequently, if not always*. The values of the choices that matched up to each construct combine to formulate the average for each construct.

The MLQ-5x contained several subscales that can be combined to arrive at scores for the different leadership types. The analysis involved combining the following subscales to measure transformational leadership: (a) idealized attributes, (b) idealized behaviors, (c) inspirational motivation, (d) intellectual stimulation, and (e) individualized consideration (Bass & Avolio, 2012).

Each of these subscales consisted of four questions. According to the operational definition for the present study, transformational leadership equated to the average score across the 20 questions that comprised the five subscales.

The transactional leadership score depended on answers to the following MLQ-5x subscales: (a) contingent rewards and (b) management by exception (active). Both subscales consisted of four questions each. The average across the eight items equated to the score for transactional leadership.

The final management style considered was passive/avoidant, as measured by combining the following subscales: (a) management by exception (passive) and (b) laissez-faire. Both again consisted of four questions each, yielding a total of eight questions on the MLQ-5x. The MLQ-5x combined the questions to constitute the complete scale. The score for passive/avoidant leadership equated to the average across these eight items.

Determination of the scores to input in the model for each leadership style required the average of the subscales across each leadership style. For each respondent, these scores determined an average score for transformational, transactional, and passive/avoidant leadership traits. The higher score indicated the dominant trait than the lower score.

The Job Satisfaction Survey (JSS) is a measurement tool designed by Paul Spector. Spector (2011) allows researchers to use his survey for non-commercial educational or research purposes as long as the researchers share their results with him. The Job Satisfaction Survey assesses how employees feel about their job and assesses their attitudes towards aspects of their job (Spector, 2011). The questionnaire yielded an overall job satisfaction scale that used all of the items in the survey (Spector, 2011). The researcher scored nine facets on the basis of a subset of the questions (Spector, 2011). These facets were satisfaction with pay, promotion, supervision, fringe benefits, contingent rewards, operating conditions, coworkers, nature of work, and communication (Spector, 2011).

Following Spector's (2011) instructions, the researcher initially measured job satisfaction as the average score across all 36 items. As each item response corresponded to a 6-point Likert scale, the resulting average fell between 1 and 6 (Spector, 2011).

Spector (2011) included some negatively worded items; these required reverse coding before calculating the average.

Spector (2011) also noted it is possible to divide scores between *satisfied* and *dissatisfied*. Spector's recommended approach is to code average scores from one to three as dissatisfied, from three to four as *ambivalent*, and from four through six as *satisfied*. To allow for the use of logistic regression, the *ambivalent* category required demarcation of a half point such that those scoring 3.5 and above qualified as *satisfied,* and those below 3.5 qualified as *dissatisfied.*

The researcher coded the responses from a brief demographic survey using the following dummy variables: gender as 0 for males and 1 for females, tenure status as 0 for non-tenured and 1 for tenured, and ethnicity as 0 for Caucasian and 1 for non-Caucasian (i.e., racial or ethnic minority).

Data Collection Technique

The researcher used Survey Monkey polling platform for collecting the responses to survey questions since the developers of this venue offered this software free to the public, and it was easily accessible. The researcher inserted the survey questions from the Multifactor Leadership Questionairre-5X, Job Satisfaction Survey, and Demographic Survey into Survey Monkey. The purpose of the demographic survey was to gather information on gender, tenure status, and ethnicity.

The invitation to participate in the survey informed participants they had four weeks to complete the survey, with a reminder email sent after the first week and third week sent to faculty members initially invited to participate in the survey. The researcher then exported the polled data into the statistical software SPSS for analysis. The survey displayed demographic questions first, followed by the job satisfaction questions, and then lastly the leadership style questions. The researcher expected this ordering to eliminate potential bias in the participants' responses. Conversely, answering the leadership questions before responding to job satisfaction questions would possibly predispose respondents to allowing the leadership issues to influence responses to job satisfaction. Participants could not backtrack to responded answers.

Data Organization Techniques

The researcher used Survey Monkey software to collect data then exported it into an SPSS file (Faul et al., 2009). The data organization and tracking features allow researchers to download results in a variety of formats. De-identified data was stored on an external hard drive located in a safe place for a period of five years, and then disposed of it by deleting the file.

Data Analysis Technique

Survey Monkey software provided an export feature to create a file that imported data into the Statistical Package for Social Sciences software (SPSS). The researcher used SPSS to analyze the data. First, using the demographic data, descriptive statistics were applied to determine how the participants related to the questions of gender, tenure status, and ethnicity. Second, a reliability analysis was conducted on the two instruments to ensure an acceptable amount of measurement error in the scales for the population of interest. Then Cronbach's alpha was reported. If the numbers came in below .75, the researcher removed individual items that reduced the reliability. After achieving a satisfactory level of reliability, scale scores were calculated by averaging the constituent items.

The primary hypothesis sought to determine the possibility of predicting the probability of being satisfied versus unsatisfied on the basis of each independent variable. With a dichotomous variable, logistic regression was more appropriate than multiple linear regression (Kawada & Yoshimura, 2012). The job satisfaction literature used logistic regression extensively as a statistical method appropriate for dichotomous dependent variables such as *satisfied* versus *dissatisfied* (Kawada & Yoshimura, 2012; Morrow, McElroy, & Scheibe, 2012); Villotti, Corbiere, Zaniboni, & Fraccaroli, 2012). The purpose of the method was to find how strongly an independent variable affected the probability of observing a success (i.e., an outcome coded 1 rather than 0) after controlling for other possible confounding variables. Although qualifying as a nonlinear model of probabilities, the logistic regression equation consists of a linear model of the log *odds of being satisfied* over *odds of being dissatisfied* (Siemsen & Roth, 2010). In other words, this model defines odds as the ratio of the probability of being satisfied to the probability of being dissatisfied. The model states the logistic regression equation thus:

$$\log\left(\frac{\text{pr (satisfied)}}{1 - \text{pr (satisfied)}}\right) = \alpha + \beta_1(\text{transformational leadership})$$

$$+ \beta_2(\text{transactional leadership}) + \beta_3(\text{passive/avoidant leadership})$$

$$+ \beta_4(\text{gender}) + \beta_5(\text{tenure status}) + \beta_6(\text{ethnicity})$$

The coefficients can be interpreted in terms of odds ratios, which represent the amount of change in the odds given a unit change in the independent variable. The researcher raised e (the base of natural logarithm) to the power of the coefficient in order to find the odds ratio. For example, if β_1 were equal to .25, then the odds ratio would be $e^{.25} = 1.284$. This indicates for each increase of one on the transformational leadership style score the odds of reporting satisfaction would increase by 28.4%. Note that an odds ratio greater than one implies the odds of reporting satisfaction have increased in the independent variable, while an odds ratio between 0 and 1 indicates the odds have decreased. An odds ratio equal to one exactly implies no change.

The researcher tested the coefficients for significance using a t test. Dividing the coefficient by its standard error produced a *t* statistic that could be evaluated along with the *t* distribution to determine if the coefficient differed significantly from 0. A significance level of .05 for a two-tailed test to classify significance was used.

Each estimated coefficient can be interpreted as the expected change in the log odds for a one-unit change in the respective independent variable while holding the other variables constant. This interpretation makes it possible to take into account possible overlapping effects of other variables in the model, thereby controlling for possible rival explanations. The researcher anticipated those scoring higher on the transformational leadership scale would more likely express satisfaction with their jobs. If, however, females were to show more likelihood to qualify as transformational leaders *and* were more likely to express satisfaction with their jobs, this would indicate the possibility of a spurious bivariate relationship between transformational leadership and job satisfaction. Gender was included in the model, which controlled for this possibility.

The model was evaluated both for the significance of the coefficients and the overall model fit.

The researcher presented the odds ratios (that is, exp[beta]) along with standard errors and p-values and tested each of the null hypotheses using the respective odds ratios and p-values. The researcher rejected the null hypotheses if a p-value of less than .05 resulted.

The researcher evaluated the model for overall fit. SPSS reports several pseudo-R^2s as logistic regression analogs to the "variance explained" R^2 of multiple regression (Siemsen & Roth, 2010). These can range in value from 0 (bad model fit) to 1 (perfect model fit). For completeness, the researcher reported all three. After fitting the regression model, I any non-significant predictors were dropped then the model was refit. The researcher examined the model's goodness of fit to determine if dropping the non-significant variables in any way altered the model fit.

The study identified the predominant leadership style according to the leadership scale yielding the highest value. If a respondent scored a 3.25 on the transformational leadership scale, a 4.2 on the transactional leadership scale, and a 2.8 on the passive/avoidant scale, then the style for that respondent's supervisor was transactional. Identifying the most salient scale made it possible to determine which leadership style was associated with the most satisfied faculty member. This allowed for answering the primary research questions of the leadership style-satisfaction relationship and complemented the logistic regression models that answered the sub-questions.

Reliability and Validity

At every stage of their research, researchers should actively anticipate and address each dilemma that may occur (Henderson, 2011). Variations in the planned protocol can affect reliability and validity, so the researcher reviewed any necessary or unavoidable changes in light of their potential effect on reliability and validity. The data collection instruments show consistent psychometric properties. The developers of both instruments normed the surveys on a variety of populations. This helps allay internal validity concerns that the survey measures might not assess the concepts considered the focus of the proposed study.

Reliability

Reliability refers to the consistency of a measure when given repeatedly under the same conditions (Fowler, 2008). If a scale has high reliability, then it will yield the same result today as it would yield tomorrow. The reliability of the scale does not suffer from a great degree of measurement errors, or so-called noise, which would cause the scale to yield inconsistent results on repeated applications.

Researchers applied the two instruments extensively in other contexts, suggesting researchers consider their reliability acceptable. Several published studies affirm the reliability and construct validity of the MLQ instrument (Bass et al., 2006; Muenjohn & Armstrong, 2008). Likewise, past studies have thoroughly evaluated the job satisfaction survey for psychometric properties (Spector, 2011), with reliability scores consistently above .75.

When presenting the results, the researcher reported Cronbach's alphas for the scales and subscales used to answer the research question. Assuming that university faculty members are not a unique population relative to other groups to which past researchers have applied these scales, the researcher expected the reliabilities to exceed .75. Three of the scales – transformational leadership, passive/avoidant leadership, and job satisfaction - had high reliabilities, as presented in Chapter 3. The transactional leadership scale had a reliability of only .622 for the dataset used. The researcher removed two items from the transactional leadership scale in order to improve the reliability. Removing these two questions, which are identified in Chapter 3, increased the reliability score to a more acceptable .758.

Validity

Internal validity refers to the confidence with which the researcher can state the hypothesized causal mechanism has produced variation on the dependent variable (Fowler, 2008). External validity refers to the extent to which the findings generalize to other samples in different contexts (Fowler, 2008). Researchers often find a trade-off between the two (Fowler, 2008). According to Fowler, an experimental setting gives the researcher strong control over the intervention, and hence high confidence the independent variable indeed produced change in the dependent variable. On the other hand, Fowler (2008) also stated artificial laboratory settings allow less clarity in social science research.

Since this study utilized observational data, it showed relatively high external validity as compared to its internal reliability (Fowler, 2008). In terms of internal validity, it is not possible to randomly assign one half of the sample to a transactional leader group and the other to a transformational leader group (Fowler, 2008). Thus, the causal arrow must be assumed to point from leadership style to job satisfaction. The emphasis is on the word *assumed*, since correlational studies are notoriously weak in their ability to demonstrate causation (Kawada & Yoshimura, 2012). Nonetheless, the alternative scenario – that job satisfaction among employees determines leadership styles – seemed less likely to be true. The researcher acknowledges limits to the internal validity, and may justifiably deem the causal inferences drawn from the results as fairly strong (Fowler, 2008).

With a sample drawn from a public university in Florida, the results may generalize to other public universities in Florida, as they are part of the same state system. For private schools, with their own sources of funding and their own campus cultures, the results may not generalize.

The research should be of interest to academic researchers who study the correlates of job satisfaction, but key stakeholders – such as university faculty and administrators – may also be interested in how the findings can contribute to improving the work environment and faculty retention. The researcher will present the findings in two ways, each appropriate for the respective target audience. In the case of researchers, the results are presented through the usual avenues for disseminating research findings, namely through conference presentations and journal articles. The researcher expects the discussion of these findings presented for researchers will be longer and more technical in presentation than the papers presented to professional stakeholders. In the latter case, an executive summary consisting of 1-2 pages outlining key results and recommendations will be made available to university employees who have interest. The purpose of the executive summary is to provide concise and applicable suggestions for improving job satisfaction rates on the basis of the findings.

Transition and Summary

The researcher intended for this study design to reveal how perceived leadership styles, as perceived by faculty, impact job satisfaction among university faculty. This chapter described the sample and data collection methods, which involved sampling university faculty and administering surveys analyzed quantitatively. The researcher analyzed responses by correlating different subscales from the MLQ leadership instrument with job satisfaction as well as through logistic regression. In this chapter, the reliability of the instruments was reviewed and the trade-off between internal and external validity discussed. In the next chapter, the researcher turn to the results of the analysis.

CHAPTER 3
Application to Professional Practice
and Implications for Change

In this chapter, the findings of the study are outlined, the applications to professional practice described, implications for social change are examined, and recommendations for actions are offered. The researcher concluded with recommendations for action, recommendations for further research, and personal reflections.

Overview of Study

The purpose of this correlational study was to examine the relationship between perceived academic administrator leadership styles and job satisfaction of full-time faculty members. The design of the study was correlational and nonexperimental. The independent variables were the transformational, transactional, and passive/avoidant leadership styles of academic administrators as evaluated by faculty members. The dependent variable was job satisfaction of full-time faculty members.

The researcher sought to answer the following primary research question and secondary questions:

Primary Research Question 1: What is the relationship between perceived administrator leadership styles and job satisfaction of faculty members?

Secondary Research Question 2: What is the relationship between perceived transformational leadership styles and job satisfaction of faculty members?

Secondary Research Question 3: What is the relationship between perceived transactional leadership styles and job satisfaction of faculty members?

Secondary Research Question 4: What is the relationship between perceived passive/avoidant leadership styles and job satisfaction of faculty members?

The researcher answered the research questions by testing the following hypotheses:

$H1_o$: There is no significant relationship between leadership styles and job satisfaction of faculty members.

H1a: There is a significant relationship between leadership styles and job satisfaction of faculty members.

H2o: There is no significant relationship between perceived transformational leadership styles and job satisfaction of faculty members.

H2a: There is a significant relationship between perceived transformational leadership styles and job satisfaction of faculty members.

H3o: There is no significant relationship between perceived transactional leadership styles and job satisfaction of faculty members.

H3a: There is a significant relationship between perceived transaction leadership styles and job satisfaction of faculty members.

H4o: There is no significant relationship between perceived passive/avoidant leadership styles and job satisfaction of faculty members.

H4a: There is a significant relationship between perceived passive/avoidant leadership styles and job satisfaction of faculty members.

The findings were that at the .05 significance level, leadership style is associated with faculty job satisfaction. First, faculty whose administrators' leadership style was transformational were highly likely to be satisfied, whereas faculty with passive/avoidant leaders tended to be dissatisfied. The transactional leadership style scores varied across the job satisfaction scale, though with more dissatisfied than satisfied faculty. The researcher answered the primary research question and found support for the corresponding alternative hypothesis. Analyses of the logistic regression models that considered only one leadership style at a time answered all of the secondary research questions by testing for significance at the .05 level. The rejection of each of the null hypotheses resulted in acceptance of the corresponding alternative hypotheses that a significant relationship does exist between leadership style and job satisfaction.

Presentation of the Findings

The presentation of findings includes descriptive statistics to describe the demographics of the sample as well as the averages for participant responses to scale items. Reliability tests confirmed the adequacy of the scales used. Results of the data analysis to answer the research questions and test the hypotheses are in written descriptions as well as in table format.

Descriptive Statistics for Sample Population

The researcher received survey responses from 104 faculty members whose demographics are summarized in Table 1. Of the respondents, 52.9% (n = 55) were male, while 47.1% (n = 49) were female. Most of the respondents (93.3%, n = 97) were Caucasian; the remainder (6.7%, n = 7) were grouped together in the non-Caucasian category. More than half, 62.5% (n = 65), had tenure, while the remaining 37.5% (n = 39) did not.

Males were overrepresented in the sample relative to their numbers in the population. Among all faculty, 45% (N = 256) are male, whereas 55% (N = 311) are female. In addition, non-Caucasian respondents are underrepresented, with the percentage of non-Caucasian faculty in the population being 16.9% (N = 96). Finally, tenured faculty members were overrepresented in the sample. The percentage of tenured faculty in the population was 47% (N = 268), whereas 53% (N = 299) were not tenured.

Table 1 – Sample Demographics

Variable	Frequency	Percent
Gender		
Male	55	52.9
Female	49	47.1
Ethnicity		
Non-Caucasian	7	6.7
Caucasian	97	93.3
Tenure status		
Non-tenured	39	37.5
Tenured	65	62.5

Note. N = 104.

Although the sample did not perfectly represent the population, the effects of these deviations from the population distributions were minimal for the statistical models reported. The final results table presented a model that estimated the leadership-satisfaction connection while controlling for these demographics. The coefficients represent the size of the effect under study, not affected by any differences in gender, ethnicity, or tenure status.

Reliability Tests of Scales

The researcher invited respondents to complete the MLQ-5 and job satisfaction surveys. The MLQ-5 survey contained several subscales covering different types of leadership styles including transformational, transactional, and passive/avoidant (Bass & Avolio, 2012). Table 2 contains the calculated reliabilities for each of the subscales along with the reliability for the undivided job satisfaction scale. The type of reliability reported is Cronbach's alpha. Cronbach's alpha is a measure that varies from 0 to 1. This reliability measurement indicates the extent to which the individual scale items are consistently measuring the same concept (Fowler, 2008). Low levels of alpha mean that the scale contains quite a bit of error, while levels that approach 1 indicate that the scale measures the concept with relatively little error. Three of the scales – transformational leadership, passive/avoidant leadership, and job satisfaction – have high reliabilities.

Table 2 – Scale Reliabilities

Scale Reliabilities	
Scale	Cronbach's Alpha
Transformational leadership	0.974
Transactional leadership (Full)	0.622
Transactional leadership (Short)	0.758
Passive/avoidant leadership	0.900
Job satisfaction	0.944

The highest value of Cronbach's alpha is .974 for transformational leadership, followed by .944 for the job satisfaction scale, and .900 for the passive/avoidant scale. The transactional leadership scale, however, had a reliability of only .622 for the dataset used. I removed two items from the transactional leadership scale in order to improve the reliability. These items were (a) MLQ.35— Expresses satisfaction when others meet expectations and (b) MLQ.24—Keeps track of all mistakes. Removing the two questions increased the reliability score to a more acceptable .758. I used this shortened version of the transactional leadership scale in the analysis that follows.

Descriptive Statistics for Responses to Scale Items

Table 3 contains the summary statistics for the scales that result from taking means across the constituent scale items. The transformational leadership scale ranges from 1.16 up to 5.0 with a mean of 3.771 (SD = 1.013). The short version of the transactional leadership scale (after dropping the two items) ranged from 1.0 to 4.75 with a mean of 1.904 (SD = .883).

Table 3 – Scale Descriptive Statistics

Scale	Min	Max	*M*	*SD*
Transformational leadership	1.16	5.00	3.771	1.013
Transactional leadership (Short)	1.00	4.75	1.904	0.883
Passive/avoidant leadership	1.50	5.00	3.332	0.814
Job satisfaction	1.00	5.00	3.942	1.295

Scores on the passive/avoidant scale ranged from 1.50 up to 5.0 with an average of 3.332 (*SD* = .814). The job satisfaction scale ranged from 1 to 5 with an average of 3.942 (*SD* = 1.295). In the statistical analysis that follows, I dichotomized job satisfaction scores such that values greater than 3.5 indicated satisfaction and values less than or equal to 3.5 indicated dissatisfaction. As reflected in Table 4, this categorical coding of job satisfaction resulted in 67.3% (*n* = 70) of respondents falling into the satisfied category, while the remaining 32.7% (*n* = 34) fell into the dissatisfied category.

*Table 4 – Job Satisfaction and Dominant Leadership
Type*

Variable Categories	Frequency	Percent
Job satisfaction		
Satisfied	34	32.7
Dissatisfied	70	67.3
Dominant leadership type		
Transformational	79	76.0
Transactional	8	7.7
Passive/avoidant	12	11.5
Multiple	5	4.8

In addition, a dominant leadership style variable emerged by identifying the leadership scale having the highest score. By far the most dominant style reported was transformational, which was the scale with the highest value for 76% (n = 79) of respondents. The second most common was passive/avoidant, which was the dominant type reported for 11.5% (n = 12) of respondents. Least common was transactional leadership, with only 7.7% (n = 8) of the sample reporting this type of leadership as most dominant. The remaining 4.8% (n = 5) of respondents did not identify a single identifiable salient leadership type.

Primary Research Question Data Analysis and Outcomes

The researcher answered the primary research question on the relationship between perceived administrator leadership styles and job satisfaction of faculty members. Prior to answering the specific secondary questions related to each of the leadership styles, and Figure 1 displays the levels of job satisfaction by the dominant leadership type as identified in Table 4. The numbers along the vertical axis correspond to the percentage of subjects in the respective dominant leadership group that fell into each satisfaction category.

The figure shows a clear pattern. No subjects who identified passive/avoidant as the dominant leadership style fell into the satisfied category. On the other hand, most of the respondents who identified transformational leadership as the dominant style fell into the satisfied category. Specifically, 15.2% ($n = 12$) of employees with transformational supervisors were dissatisfied, while the other 84.8% ($n = 67$) were satisfied. The employees with transactional leaders tended to be dissatisfied, though some did fall into the

satisfied category. Of these respondents, 75% (*n* = 6)
were dissatisfied, while the remaining 25% (*n* = 2) were
satisfied.

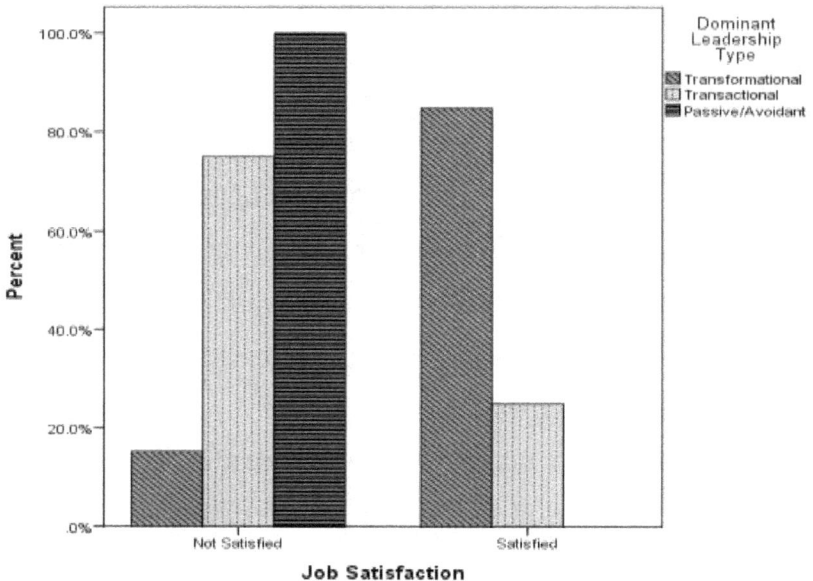

Figure 1. Job satisfaction by dominant leadership type

A chi-square test of independence showed these
differences are statistically significant (χ^2 = 43.711, *df* =
2, *p* < .001). The effect size, Cramer's *V*, was .664,
which is large according to conventional standards
(Fowler, 2008). Job satisfaction appears to vary with
leadership style in a manner that is both statistically and

substantively significant, so the null hypothesis was rejected for Primary Research Question 1.

Secondary Research Questions Data Analysis and Outcomes

The previous analysis for the primary research question offers evidence for an affirmative answer and rejection of the null hypothesis of the primary research question. The relationship between each individual leadership subscale and satisfaction were examined to answer the remaining secondary questions. Tables 5 and 6 present results of logistic regression models. In these models, the dichotomized job satisfaction variable is the outcome and the different leadership styles are predictors. The tables also display the effects of demographics on job satisfaction.

Table 5 reflects the bivariate relationships and presents results of separate models that include each predictor as the sole independent variable. The intent is to demonstrate the unadjusted relationship that is present before controlling for other confounders. Table 6 then includes all of the variables simultaneously. The purpose of Table 6 results was to answer the following questions: (a) does one leadership style dominate the others in predicting job satisfaction, and (b) do significant bivariate relationships existing between leadership style and satisfaction disappear after controlling for demographics?

Table 5 first presents the bivariate relationships. The bivariate relationships between each of the leadership styles and job satisfaction were highly significant. The coefficients in the table are the untransformed coefficients from the logistic regression model that represent the amount of expected change in the log of the odds of satisfaction for a one-unit change in the predictor (Fowler, 2008). The standard errors correspond to these untransformed coefficients from the logistic regression model. The Wald test evaluated whether the coefficient of the null hypothesis is 0, and the p-value column showed the significance of the test. The final column contains odds ratios, which is an interpretable transformation of the coefficient. Odds ratios greater than one mean that, for each unit increase in the independent variable, the odds of being satisfied increase by 100*(odds ratio − 1)%. Odds ratios less than one indicated that the odds of being satisfied decrease by 100*(1 − odds ratio)%.

Table 5 – Logistic Regressions: Single Independent Variable

Variable	B	SE	Wald	df	p	OR
Gender (female = 1)	.179	.420	.182	1	.670	1.196
Ethnicity (non-Caucasian = 1)	1.091	.795	1.885	1	.170	2.978
Tenure (non-tenured = 1)	-.332	.440	.569	1	.451	.717
Transformational leadership	4.109***	.968	18.017	1	.000	60.905
Transactional leadership (short)	2.552***	.506	25.426	1	.000	12.831
Passive/avoidant leadership	-2.310***	.440	27.633	1	.000	.099

Note. Each row is a separate logit model containing only the respective predictor.
*** $p < .001$

Demographics. The results showed that demographics do not appear to matter as predictors of satisfaction. According to the last column in Table 5, the odds of being satisfied were 19.6% higher for females compared to males, but this was not statistically significant ($B = .179$, $SE = .420$, $p = .670$). In addition, the odds of being satisfied were nearly three times higher for non-Caucasians compared to Caucasians, but this was again non-significant when compared to

Caucasians (B = 1.091, SE = .795, p = .170. The odds
of being satisfied were 28.3% lower for non-tenured
faculty, but the difference was not significant (B = -.332,
SE = .440, p = .451). Although the sample is not
perfectly representative, the effects of these deviations
from the population distributions were minimal for the
statistical models reported below because the model
controlled for these variables. The final results table
reflects data for a model that estimated the leadership-
satisfaction connection while controlling for these
demographics.

Secondary Research Question 2. In secondary
research question 2, the researcher asked whether there
is a significant relationship between transformational
leadership styles and faculty member job satisfaction.
For each one-unit increase on the transformational
leadership scale, the odds of being satisfied increased
60-fold, an effect that was clearly significant (B = 4.109,
SE = .968, p < .001). Therefore, the null hypothesis was
rejected for this research question.

Secondary Research Question 3. In secondary
research question 3, the researcher asked whether there

is a significant relationship between transactional
leadership styles and faculty member job satisfaction.
The size of the bivariate relationship between
transactional leadership and job satisfaction was not
quite as substantial as with transformational leadership,
though it was still large. Each unit increase on the
transactional leadership scale leads to a nearly 13-fold
increase in the odds of being satisfied. The result was
again highly significant (B = 2.552, SE = .506, p < .001).
Therefore, the null hypothesis was rejected for this
research question.

Secondary Research Question 4. In secondary
research question 4, the researcher asked whether there
is a significant relationship between passive/avoidant
leadership styles and faculty member job satisfaction.
Once again, the result was highly significant (B = -2.310,
SE = .440, p < .001). Each unit increase on the
passive/avoidant scale leads to a 90% decrease in the
odds of being satisfied. Therefore, the null hypothesis
was rejected for this research question.

Multivariate relationships. The results
displayed in Table 6 reflect the full model which

simultaneously included all of the independent variables. Using a two-sided alpha level of .05 as the cut-off for significance, all of the demographic variables remained non-significant. The odds ratio estimate of 23.179 for ethnicity is extremely large, but this result should be interpreted carefully given the small number of non-Caucasian respondents (see Table 1). The tenure variable approaches significance (that is, it would be significant in a one-tailed test, B = -2.331, SE = 1.265, p = .078). The odds that a non-tenured faculty member is satisfied are 89.3% lower relative to a tenured faculty member. Still, holding to the .05 significance level criterion, it is not possible to state there are significant differences in satisfaction between tenured and non-tenured faculty.

Turning to the leadership style variables, it is clear that the transformational leadership style contains most of the predictive power. Each unit increase on the transformational leadership scale lead to a 63-fold increase in the odds of being satisfied, a result that is easily significant (B = 4.150, SE = 1.429, p = .004).

Table 6 – Logistic Regression: Full Model

Variable	B	SE	Wald	df	p	OR
Gender (female = 1)	.620	.952	.425	1	.514	1.860
Ethnicity (non-Caucasian = 1)	3.143	1.804	3.034	1	.082	23.179
Tenure (non-tenured = 1)	-2.231	1.265	3.114	1	.078	.107
Transformational leadership	4.150**	1.429	8.438	1	.004	63.412
Transactional leadership (Short)	-.754	.630	1.432	1	.231	.471
Passive/avoidant leadership	.101	1.080	.009	1	.926	1.106
Constant	-15.343	5.780	7.047	1	.008	.000
Nagelkerke R^2	0.823					
Cox & Snell R^2	0.590					

At the same time, the other two leadership types
lost their significance, and their coefficients even reverse
sign (transactional leadership: B = -.754, SE = .630, p =
.231; passive/avoidant: B = .101, SE = 1.080, p = .926).
The change in sign was likely attributable to the fact that
transformational leadership accounted for any
relationship previously observed between these other
leadership types and job satisfaction. Thus, controlling
for transformational leadership, the true relationship

between the other leadership types and job satisfaction is 0, and the coefficient estimates reflected nothing more than sampling variability. The model fit statistics were quite large. The Nagelkerke R2 is .823, and the Cox and Snell R2 was .590 (Fowler, 2008). These measures are analogues to the R2 from linear regression (Fowler, 2008), and as such they indicated extremely high predictive power on the basis of the model.

Summary of Results

In the primary research question, I asked what the relationship is between administrator leadership styles and faculty member job satisfaction. Regarding dominant leadership types, clearly the respondents working under transformational leaders were most satisfied. Respondents working under passive/avoidant leaders were least satisfied. These differences were statistically and substantively significant according to a chi-square test (Fowler, 2008). This result confirms past research claiming that the most effective leaders use both transformational and transactional leadership (Bass & Riggio, 2006; Yukl & Mahsud, 2010).

By far the most dominant style reported was transformational, and the second most dominant style reported was transactional. This confirms an earlier finding by Jones and Rudd's (2008) survey that as a group the deans or program directors in colleges and universities tended to prefer transformational leadership, also making use of transactional leadership. Leaders in Jones and Rudd's (2008) study exhibited the transactional leadership style least often, as is true for the passive/avoidant leadership style in the present study.

Examining the relationship between the leadership style scales and job satisfaction, the bivariate results showed that the unadjusted associations were significant for all leadership types. Higher scores on transformational and transactional leadership scales increased the odds of being satisfied, while higher scores on the passive/avoidant scale meant less satisfaction than transformational or transaction scores. Demographics did not appear to matter.

Examining a full multivariate model, transformational leadership reflected as the dominant predictor of job satisfaction. Rowold and Scholtz (2009) study exhibited this same outcome, with transformational leadership as the dominant factor in relating to job satisfaction. Both transactional and passive/avoidant leadership lost their significance after controlling for transformational leadership, whereas the transformational leadership style remained a statistically and substantively significant predictor of job satisfaction.

Applications for Professional Practice

Faculty members play a vital role in the success of higher education institutions (Cordeiro, 2010). Increased job satisfaction and better retention of faculty reduce the need for costly faculty selection and hiring, and higher retention adds financial stability to the institution (Froesche & Sinkford, 2009). Faculty job satisfaction and its relationship to retention in higher education are business related issues, as a 5% increase in retention can lead to a 10% reduction in costs (Wong & Heng, 2009). A similar increase in retention can further result in substantial productivity increases, to as much as 65% (Wong & Heng, 2009).

University leaders represent a crucial element of job satisfaction (Wong & Heng, 2009), and consequently, they directly affect faculty turnover in higher education institutions. As the State University System of Florida is in the process of launching the New Florida Initiative, enrollments will likely increase across all universities within the system (State University System of Florida, 2012). This increased enrollment may result in rapid transformation of leadership positions because of the need for larger numbers teaching faculty (Lawrence & Bell, 2012). As this happens, faculty leaders will have greater responsibility and/or create more faculty leadership positions. This creates an opportunity for top college and university administrators to (a) communicate the expectation that leaders cultivate faculty job satisfaction and (b) assist faculty leaders in this effort by instructing them regarding research-based effective leadership models.

The results of the study indicated higher scores on the transformational and transactional leadership scales increased the odds of faculty members of the university being satisfied while higher scores on the passive/avoidant leadership scale decreased the odds of the faculty being satisfied. Therefore, the results of this study provided a model for administrators to predict how their leadership styles will impact job satisfaction of faculty members.

Implications for Social Change

Whether the results of a study closes the existing research and practice depends upon the degree of a research study's significance for practical application. Higher education is one of the central drivers of positive social change, and the quality of social progress directly depends upon the quality of higher education in the United States (Billiger & Wasilik, 2009). Study results identified effective leadership models in higher education and raises public awareness of their importance in public state universities. This knowledge enables higher education professionals to enhance their leadership style decisions and, consequently, drive positive social change. Faculty of higher education institutions perform vital functions in society. The faculty can cultivate aptitudes and attitudes in the brightest young minds that can foster needed cultural change in society. Faculty can do this most effectively when their department heads provide responsive leadership that enables them to employ their ideas and talents.

Recommendations for Action

The results of this study showed the significance of the relationship between transformational, transactional, and passive/avoidant leadership styles and job satisfaction. These results may be of interest to academic researchers who study the correlates of job satisfaction, but key stakeholders, such as university faculty and administrators, may also be interested in how the findings can contribute to improving the work environment and faculty retention. The researcher will present the findings in two ways, each appropriate for the respective target audience. In the case of researchers, the researcher will present the results through the usual avenues for disseminating research findings, namely through conference presentations and journal articles. It is expected the discussion of these findings presented for researchers will be longer and more technical in presentation than the papers presented to professional stakeholders.

In the case of university faculty and administrators, the researcher will make available an executive summary consisting of one to two pages outlining key results and recommendations to university employees who express interest. The executive summary purpose is to provide quick and easily digestible advice for improving job satisfaction rates on the basis of the findings.

Academic leaders may take further action by refining their leadership styles on the basis of their faculty members' indicated preferences. This refinement may help to achieve the highest possible satisfaction rates among the faculty members. Based on analysis, transformational leadership is very likely a key determinant for improving job satisfaction for this population of faculty members.

Vecchio et al. (2008) used path-goal theory to explore the potential of transformational and transactional leadership models to predict performance satisfaction among followers. Under these leadership models, leaders exercise transactional contingent reward leadership by gaining influence through the use of external incentives that are contingent on followers' performance (Vecchio et al., 2008). According to path-goal theory, the leader's role includes enriching the environment when the existing rewards are inadequate (Vecchio et al., 2008). Vecchio found that the effects of transactional leadership exceeded the influence of

transformational leadership, yet their findings also
showed that the leader's vision and intellectual
stimulation had greater influence in situations with
limited use of contingent reward (Vecchio et al., 2008).
In other words, in situations absent the use of extrinsic
rewards, the model predicts enhanced impact of
transformational leadership (Vecchio et al., 2008).

Recommendations for Further Study

The study sample included a single state
university in the State University System of Florida out of
11 state universities. Much more additional research in
the area of academic leadership and faculty job
satisfaction is warranted. First, due to the study sample,
only including a single government operated university
future researchers may explore the relationship between
academic leadership styles and faculty member job
satisfaction within 2-year community colleges or 4-year
state colleges. Alternately, future researchers may
evaluate the impact of leadership styles on faculty job
satisfaction within for-profit, private colleges and
universities. Second, the demographic questions
addressed only included three confounding variables,

which were tenure status, gender, and ethnicity. Within the model presented in this study, these variables showed no significant impact on job satisfaction. Future researchers may consider including additional demographic variables when evaluating job satisfaction among faculty members, such as teaching experience, education level, and different sub-sets of ethnicity. Finally, researchers may also wish to consider verifying the apparent assumption of the absence of interaction among the demographic variables.

Reflections

As a faculty member in the Florida College System, I have witnessed and experienced effective leadership and less effective leadership. I have noted the positive and negative impacts of leadership actions and styles. These observations led me to this research interest and motivated me to disseminate the research findings. My affiliation with an academic institution provided credibility to me during research protocol process at the subject university. As a faculty member, my motivations and values were understood to align with those of the university. If personal biases or preconceived ideas existed, the possible effects thereof were minimized or negated based on the fact the participants had no direct contact with me, but instead completed online questionnaires anonymously. By conducting a quantitative study, no personal interpretation of ambiguous statements were of concern; rather, the quantitative analysis is more robust to the potential effects of personal interpretations of respondents' than would qualitative studies. The results of the study were not surprising to me personally as they are in line with expectations based on the existing body of leadership literature and research, such as Herold et al.'s (2008) findings of the positive effects of transformational leadership.

Summary and Study Conclusions

In this quantitative correlational study, I explored the relationship between perceived academic administrator leadership styles and job satisfaction of full-time faculty members. The independent variables were the perceived transformational, transactional, and passive/avoidant leadership styles of academic administrators as evaluated by 104 faculty member respondents from a Florida university. The dependent variable was job satisfaction of full-time faculty members. Demographic analysis showed the respondents to be roughly evenly distributed between male and female respondents, largely Caucasian (i.e., not of a minority racial or ethnic category), and comprised of roughly twice as many tenured as compared to non-tenured respondents. Respondents identified the dominant leadership styles of their direct administrator in their institution. Results were that the most dominant style was transformational, as identified by 76% of respondents as most dominant; followed by passive/avoidant, as identified by 11.5% of respondents as most dominant; then transactional leadership, as identified by only 7.7% of the sample as most dominant. The study results showed that (a) most of the respondents who identified transformational leadership as the dominant style had high job satisfaction (84.8%); (b) the respondents who identified transactional leadership as the dominant style had high job satisfaction (25%), and (c) no respondents who identified passive/avoidant leadership as the dominant style had high job satisfaction.

This research study finding formed the basis of the recommendations that academic leaders take a proactive position by (a) disseminating this information and (b) refining their leadership styles on the basis of their faculty members' indicated preferences. Thus, academic leaders may enable themselves to achieve the highest possible job satisfaction rates among their faculty members. It is critical universities retain satisfied employees to enhance productivity and maintain sound financial standing (Cordeiro, 2010). This strong financial standing allows for the institution's leadership to offer affordable tuition, compete effectively in attracting quality students, and maintain or enhance their standing among higher education institutions. Stakeholders can use the results of this study to create a strategy that will help them to increase faculty satisfaction, and thereby, increase faculty and university effectiveness.

REFERENCES

Akroyd, D., Bracken, S., & Chambers, C. (2011). A comparison of
factors that predict the satisfaction of community college faculty
by gender. *Journal of the Professoriate, 4*(1), 74-95. Retrieved
from http://jotp.icbche.org

Ambrose, S., Huston, T., & Norman, M. (2005). A qualitative method
for assessing faculty satisfaction. *Research in Higher
Education, 46*(7), 803-830. doi:10.1007/s11162-004-6226-6

Apostolou, B., Hassell, J. M., Rebele, J. E., &Watson, S. F. (2010).
Accounting education literature review (2006-2009). *Journal of
Accounting Education, 28*(3/4), 145-197.
doi:10.1016/j.bbr.2011.03.031

Austin, A. E. (2012). Challenges and visions for higher education in
a complex world: Commentary on Barnett and Barrie. *Higher
Education Research & Development, 31*(1), 57-64.
doi:10.1080/07294360.2012.642840

Ayman, R., & Korabik, K. (2010). Leadership: Why gender and
culture matter. *American Psychologist, 65*(3), 157-170.
doi:10.1037/a0018806

Baker, S. L., Fitzpatrick, J. J., & Griffin, M. Q. (2011). Empowerment
and job satisfaction in associate degree nurse educators. *Nurse
Education Perspectives, 32*(4), 234-239. doi:10.5480/1536-
5026-32.4.234

Bass, B. M., Avolio, B. J., Jung, D. I., & Berson, Y. (2012).
Predicting unit performance by assessing transformational and
transactional leadership. *Journal of Applied Psychology, 88*(2),
207-218. doi:10.1037/0021-9010.88.2.207

Bass, B. M., & Riggio, R. (2006). *Transformational leadership* (2nd
ed.). Mahwah, NJ: Erlbaum.

Baxter, P., & Jack, S. (2008). Qualitative case study methodology:
Study design and implementation for novice researchers.
Qualitative Report, 13(4), 554-559. Retrieved from
http://www.nova.edu

Belli, G. (2008). *Nonexperimental quantitative research*. Retrieved
from http://www.media.wiley.com

Bennis, W. (2010, February). Leadership competencies. *Leadership*

Excellence, 27(2), 20-21. Retrieved from
http://www.leaderexcel.com

Bilimoria, D., Joy, S., & Liang, X. (2008). Breaking barriers and
creating inclusiveness: Lessons of organizational transformation
to advance women faculty in academic science and
engineering. *Human Resource Management, 47*(3), 423-441.
doi:10.1002/hrm.20225

Bodla, M. A., & Nawaz, M. M. (2010). Transformational leadership
style and its relationship with satisfaction. *Interdisciplinary
Journal of Contemporary Research in Business, 2*(1), 370-381.
Retrieved from http://www.ijcrb.webs.com

Bolliger, D. U., & Wasilik, O. (2009). Factors influencing faculty
satisfaction with online teaching and learning in higher
education. *Distance Education, 30,* 103-116.
doi:10.1080/01587910902845949

Bozeman, B., & Gaughan, M. (2011). Job satisfaction among
university faculty: Individual, work, and institutional
determinants. *Journal of Higher Education, 82,* 154-186.
doi:10.1353/jhe.2011.0011

Campbell, D. F., Syed, S., & Morris, P. A. (2010). Minding the gap:
Filling a void in community college leadership development.
New Directions for Community Colleges, 149, 33-39.
doi:10.1002/cc.393

Castro, C. B., Perifian, M. M. V., & Bueno, C. C. (2008).
Transformational leadership and followers' attitudes: The
mediating role of psychological empowerment. *International
Journal of Human Resource Management, 19,* 1842-1863.
doi:10.1080/09585190802324601

Chung, K. C., Song, J. W., Kim, M., Wooliscroft, J. O., Quint, E. H.,
Lukacs, N. W., & Gyetko, M. R. (2010). Predictors of job
satisfaction among academic faculty: Do instructional and
clinical faculty differ? *Medical Education, 44,* 985-995.
doi:10.1111/j.1365-2923.2010.03766.x

Coates, H., Dobson, I. R., Goedegebuure, L., & Meek, L. (2010).
Across the great divide: What do Australian academics think of
university leadership? Advice from the CAP survey. *Journal of
Higher Education Policy and Management, 32,* 379-387.
doi:10.1080/1360080X.2010.491111

Cordeiro, W. P. (2010). A business school's unique hiring process.
Business Education Innovation Journal, 2(1), 56-60. Retrieved
from http://www.beijournal.com/

Cropsey, K. L., Masho, S. W., Shiang, R., Sikka, V., Kornstein, S.
G., & Hampton, C. L. (2008). Why do faculty leave? Reasons
for attrition of women and minority faculty from a medical

school: Four-year results. *Journal of Women's Health, 17,* 1111-1118. doi:10.1089/jwh.2007.0582

Cummings, G. G., MacGregor, T., Davey, M., Lee, H., Wong, C. A., Lo, E., Muise, M., & Stafford, E. (2010). Leadership styles and outcome patterns for the nursing workforce and work environment: A systematic review. *International Journal of Nursing Studies, 47*(3), 363-385. doi:10.1016/j.ijnurstu.2009.08.006

Deluga, R. J. (2011). Supervisor trust building, leader-member exchange and organizational citizenship behaviour. *Journal of Occupational and Organizational Psychology, 67*(4), 315-326. doi:10.1111/j.2044-8325.1994.tb00570.x

DeConinck, J. B. (2009). The effect of leader-member exchange on turnover among retail buyers. *Journal of Business Research, 62*(11), 1081-1086. doi:10.1016/j.jbusres.2008.09.011

Derue, D. S., Nahrgang, J. D., Wellman, N., & Humphrey, S. E. (2011). Trait and behavioral theories of leadership: An integration and meta-analytic test of their relative validity. *Personnel Psychology, 64*(1), 7-52. doi:10.1111/j.1744-6570.2010.01201.x

Faul, F., Erdfelder, E., Buchner, A., & Lang, A. G. (2009). Statistical power analyses using g* power 3.1: Tests for correlation and regression analyses. Behavior Research Methods, *41,* 1149-1160. Retrieved from http://www.psyconomic.org

Finch, J. H., Allen, R. S., & Weeks, H. S. (2010). The salary premium required for replacing management faculty: Evidence from a national survey. *Journal of Education for Business, 85,* 264-267. doi:10.1080/08832320903449576

Fowler, F. J. (2008). *Survey research methods* (4th ed.). Thousand Oaks, CA: Sage.

Froeschle, M. L., & Sinkford, J. C. (2009). Full-time dental faculty perceptions of satisfaction with the academic work environment. *Journal of Dental Education, 73,* 1153-1170. Retrieved from http://www.jdentaled.org

Fry, L., & Kriger, M. (2009). Towards a theory of being-centered leadership: Multiple levels of being as context for effective leadership. *Human Relations, 61*(11), 1667-1996. doi:10.1177/0018726709346380

Fuller, K., Maniscalco-Feichtl, M., & Droege, M. (2008). The role of the mentor in retaining junior pharmacy faculty members. *American Journal of Pharmaceutical Education, 72*(2), 1-5. doi:10.5688/aj720241

Gill, A., Mand, H. S., Culpepper, A., Mathur, N., & Bhutani, S.

(2011). The relations of transformational leadership and empowerment with student perceived academic performance: A study among Indian commerce students. *Business and Economics Journal, 34*, 1-9. Retrieved from http://www.astonjournals.com

Green, T., Alejandro, J., & Brown, A. H. (2009). The retention of experienced faculty in online distance education programs: Understanding factors that impact their involvement. *International Review of Research in Open and Distance Learning, 10*(3), 1-15. Retrieved from http://www.irrodl.org

Gutierrez, A. P., Candela, L. L., & Carver, L. (2012). The structural relationships between organizational commitment, global job satisfaction, developmental experiences, work values, organizational support, and person-organization fit among nursing faculty. *Journal of Advanced Nursing, 68*(7), 1601-1614. doi:10.1111/j.1365-2648.2012.05990.x

Henderson, K. A. (2011). Post-Positivism and the Pragmatics of Leisure Research. *Leisure Sciences, 33*(4), 341-346. doi:10.1080/01490400.2011.583166

Herold, D. M., Fedor, D. B., Caldwell, S., & Liu, Y. (2008). The effects of transformational and change leadership on employees' commitment to change: A multilevel study. *Journal of Applied Psychology, 93*, 346-357. doi:10.1037/0021-9010.93.2.346

Jing, F. F., & Avery, G. C. (2011). Missing links in understanding the relationship between leadership and organizational performance. *International Business & Economics Research Journal, 7*(5), 67-78. Retrieved from http://www.inderscience.com

Jones, D., & Rudd, R. (2008). Transactional, transformational, or laissez-faire leadership: An assessment of college of agriculture academic program leaders' (deans) leadership styles. *Journal of Agricultural Education, 49*(2), 88-97. doi:10.5032/jae.2008.02088

Judgea, T. A., Piccolob, R. F., Podsakoffc, N. P., Shawd, J. C., & Riche, B. L. (2010). The relationship between pay and job satisfaction: A meta-analysis of the literature. *Journal of Vocational Behavior, 77*(2), 157-167. doi:10.1016/j.jvb.2010.04.002

Kawada, T., & Yoshimura, M. (2012). Results of a 100-point scale for evaluating job satisfaction and the occupational depression scale questionnaire survey in workers. *Journal of Occupational and Environmental Medicine, 54*, 420-423. doi:10.1097/JOM.0b013e31824173ab

Kezar, A. (2010). Leadership for a better world: Understanding the social change model of leadership development. *The Journal of Higher Education, 81*(5), 670-671. doi:10.1353/jhe.2010.0001

Kim, D., Twombley, S., & Wolf-Wendel, L. (2008). Factors predicting community college faculty satisfaction with instructional autonomy. *Community College Review, 35*(3), 159-180. doi:10.1177/0091552107310173101011

Klein, J., & Takeda-Tinker, B. (2009). The impact of leadership on community college faculty job satisfaction. *Academic Leadership: The Online Journal, 7*(2), 1-5. Retrieved from http://www.academicleadership.org

Kouzes, J. M., & Posner, B. Z. (2007). *The leadership challenge* (4th ed.). San Francisco, CA: Jossey-Bass.

Krivokapic-Skoko, B., & O'Neill, G. (2008). University academics' psychological contracts in Australia: A mixed method research approach. *Electronic Journal of Business Research Methods, 6*(1), 61-72. Retrieved from http://www.ejbrm.com

Lawrence, J., Ott, M., & Bell, A. (2012). Faculty organizational commitment and citizenship. *Research in Higher Education, 53*(3), 325-352. doi:10.1007/s11162-011-9230-7

Leech, N. L., & Onwuegbuzie, A. J. (2011). A typology of mixed research designs. *Quantity and Quality, 43*(2), 265-275. Retrieved from http://www.springer.com

Leithwood, K., & Sun, J. (2012). The nature and effects of transformational school leadership: A meta-analytic review of unpublished research. *Educational Administration Quarterly, 48*(3), 387-423.

Lenhardt, M., Ricketts, J. C., Morgan, A. C., & Karnock, K. J. (2011). Leadership behaviors of Georgia golf course superintendents: Implications for post-secondary programs. *NACTA Journal, 55*(4), 23-30. Retrieved from http://www.nactateachers.org

Li, C-K., & Hung, C-H. (2009). The influence of transformational leadership on workplace relationships and job performance. *Social Behavior and Personality, 37*, 1129-1142. doi:10.2224/sbp.2009.37.8.1129

Mardanov, I. T., Heischmidt, K., & Henson, A. (2008). Leader-member exchange and job satisfaction bond and predicted employee turnover. *Journal of Leadership & Organizational Studies, 15*(2), 159-175. doi:10.1177/1548051808320985

Marston, S. H., & Brunetti, G. J. (2009). Job satisfaction of experienced professors at a liberal arts college. *Education, 130*(2), 323-347. Retrieved from http://www.projectinnovation.biz

Maynard, D. C., & Joseph, T. A. (2008). Are all part-time faculty underemployed? The influence of faculty status preference on satisfaction and commitment. *Higher Education, 55*(2), 139-154. doi:10.1007/s10734-006-9039-z

Miller, M. M. (2011). Improving response to web and mixed-mode surveys. *Public Opinion Quarterly, 75*(2), 249-269. doi:10.1093/poq/nfr047

Mohammad, S. I. S., Al-Zeaud, H. A., & Batayneh, A. M. E. (2011). The relationship between transformational leadership and employees' satisfaction at Jordanian private hospitals. *Business and Economic Horizons, 5*(2), 35-46. Retrieved from http://academicpublishingplatforms.com

Morrow, P., McElroy, J., & Scheibe, K. (2011). Work-unit incivility, job satisfaction, and total quality management among transportation employees. *Transportation Research Part E: Logistics and Transportation Review, 47*(6), 1210-1220. doi:10.1016/j.tre.2011.03.004

Muenjohn, N., & Armstrong, A. (2008). Evaluating the structural validity of the Multifactor Leadership Questionnaire (MLQ): Capturing the leadership factors of transformational-transactional leadership. *Contemporary Management Research, 4*(1), 3-14. Retrieved from http://www.cmr-journal.org

Newhall, S. (2012). Preparing our leaders for the future. *Strategic HR Review, 11*(1), 5-12. doi:10.1108/14754391211186250

Northouse, P. G. (2010). *Leadership: Theory and practice* (5th ed.). Thousand Oaks, CA: Sage.

Mutjaba, B. (2009). Faculty development practices in distance education for success with culturally diverse students. *International Business & Economics Research Journal, 4*(4), 1-12. Retrieved from http://www.inderscience.com

O'Meara, K. A., & Terosky, A. (2008). Faculty careers and work lives: A professional growth perspective. *ASHE Higher Education Report, 34*(3), 1-221. doi:10.1002/aehe.3403

Petersen, G., & Caplow, J. A. (2004, September). Leadership style and perceived effectiveness. *Academic Leader,* p. 5. Retrieved from http://www.facultyfocus.com

Pieterse, A. N., van Knippenberg, D., Schippers, M., Stam, D. (2010). Transformational and transactional leadership and innovative behavior: The moderating role of psychological empowerment. *Journal of Organizational Behavior, 31*(4), 609-623. doi:10.1002/job.650

Pololi, L. H., Krupat, E., Civian, J. T., Ash, A. S., & Brennan, R. T. (2012). Why are a quarter of faculty considering leaving academic medicine? A study of their perceptions of institutional culture and intentions to leave at 26 representative U.S. medical

schools. *Academic Medicine, 87*(7), 859-869.
doi:10.1097/ACM.0b013e3182582b18

Rashid, U., & Rashid, S. (2011). The effect of job enrichment on job satisfaction: A case study of faculty members. *Interdisciplinary Journal of Contemporary Research in Business, 3*(4), 106-117. Retrieved from http://www.ijcrb.webs.com

Riaz, A., & Haider, M. H. (2010). Role of transformational and transactional leadership on job satisfaction and career satisfaction. *Business and Economic Horizons, 1*(1), 29-38. Retrieved from http://www.academicpublishingplatforms.com

Reybold, L. E., Brazer, S. D., Schrum, L., & Corda, K. W. (2012). The politics of dissertation advising: How early career women faculty negotiate access and participation. *Innovative Higher Education, 37*(3), 227-242. doi:10.1007/s10755-011-9200-1

Rogotzke, K. (2011). *Iowa community college science, engineering and mathematics (SEM) faculty: Demographics and job satisfaction* (Doctoral dissertation). Available from ProQuest Dissertations & Theses database. (UMI No. 3494200)

Rosser, V. J., & Townsend, B. K. (2006). Determining public 2-year college faculty's intent to leave: An empirical model. *Journal of Higher Education, 77,* 124-147. doi:10.1353/jhe.2006.0006

Rowold, J., & Schlotz, W. (2009). Transformational and transactional leadership and followers' chronic stress, *Leadership Review, 9,* 35-48. Retrieved from http://www.leadershipreview.org

Sabharwal, M., & Corley, E. A. (2009). Faculty job satisfaction across gender and discipline. *Social Science Journal, 46*(3), 539-556. doi:10.1016/j.soscij.2009.04.015

Safi, M., Falahi Khoshknab, M., Russell, M., & Rahgozar, M. (2011). Job satisfaction among faculty members of University of Social Welfare and Rehabilitation Sciences. *IJME, 10*(4), 323-332. Retrieved from http://ijme.mui.ac.ir

Salahuddin, M. M. (2010). Generational differences impact on leadership style and organizational success. *Journal of Diversity Management, 5*(2), 1-6. Retrieved from http://www.journals.cluteonline.com

Schweitzer, G. (2009). *Quantitative versus qualitative research.* Retrieved from http://www.keltonresearch.com

Seifert, T. A., & Umbach, P. D. (2008). The effects of faculty demographic characteristics and disciplinary context on dimensions of job satisfaction. *Research in Higher Education, 49*(4), 357-381. doi:10.1007/s11162-007-9084-1

Senter, H. F. (2012). Applied linear statistical models. *Journal of the American Statistical Association, 103,* 880-886. Retrieved from http://www.amstat.tandfonline.com

Sh Shibru, B., & Darshan, G. M. (2011). Transformational leadership and its relationship with subordinate satisfaction with the leader. *Interdisciplinary Journal of Contemporary Research in Business, 3*(5), 686-697. Retrieved from http://www.ijcrb.webs.com

Siemsen, E., Roth, A., & Oliveira, P. (2010). Common method bias in regression models with linear, quadratic, and interaction effects. *Organizational Research Methods, 13*(3), 456-476. Retrieved from http://www.orm.sagepub.com

Simplicio, J. (2011). It all starts at the top: Divergent leadership styles and their impact upon a university. *Education, 132*(1), 110-114. Retrieved from http://www.projectinnovation.biz

Sirkis, J. E. (2011). Development of leadership skills in community college department chairs. *Community College Enterprise, 17*(2), 46-61. Retrieved from http://www.schoolcraft.edu

Spector, P. E. (2011). *Job satisfaction survey.* Retrieved from http://chuma.cas.usf.edu

Spivey, C. A., Chisholm-Burns, M. A., Murphy, J. E., Rice, L., & Morelli, C. (2009). Assessment and recommendations to improve pharmacy faculty satisfaction and retention. *American Journal of Health-System Pharmacy, 66*, 54-64. Retrieved from http://www.ajhp.org

Symonds, J. E., & Gorard, S. (2010). Death of mixed methods? Or the rebirth of research as a craft. *Evaluation & Research in Education, 23*(2), 121-136. doi:10.1080/09500790.2010.483514

Taylor, C. T., & Berry, T. M. (2008). A pharmacy faculty academy to foster professional growth and long-term retention of junior faculty members. *American Journal of Pharmaceutical Education, 72*(2), 1-10. Retrieved from http://www.ajpe.org

Vecchio, R. P., Justin, J. E., & Pearce, C. L. (2008). The utility of transactional and transformational leadership for predicting performance and satisfaction within a path-goal theory framework. *Journal of Occupational and Organizational Psychology, 81*, 71-82. doi:10.1348/096317907X202482

Villotti, P., Corbière, M., Zaniboni, S., & Fraccaroli, F. (2012). Individual and environmental factors related to job satisfaction in people with severe mental illness employed in social enterprises. *Work: A Journal of Prevention, Assessment and Rehabilitation, 43*(1), 33-41. doi:10.3233/WOR-2012-1445

Webb, K. (2009). Creating satisfied employees in Christian higher education: Research on leadership competencies. *Christian Higher Education, 8*, 18-31. doi:10.1080/15363750802171073

Wang, X., & Howell, J. M. (2012). A multilevel study of transformational leadership, identification, and follower outcomes. *Leadership Quarterly, 23*(5), 775-790. doi:10.1016/j.leaqua.2012.02.001

Wong, E., & Heng, T. (2009). Case study of factors influencing job satisfaction in two Malaysian universities. *International Business Research, 2*(2), 86-98. Retrieved from http://www.ibrusa.com

Xu, Y. J. (2008a). Faculty turnover: Discipline-specific attention is warranted. *Research in Higher Education, 49*(1), 40-61. doi:10.1007/s11162-007-9062-7

Xu, Y. J. (2008b). Gender disparity in STEM disciplines: A study of faculty attrition and turnover intentions. *Research in Higher Education, 49*, 607-624. doi:10.1007/s11162-008-9097-4

Yukl, G., & Mahsud, R. (2010). Why flexible and adaptive leadership is essential. *Consulting Psychology Journal: Practice and Research, 62*(2), 81-93. doi:10.1037/a0019835

Zembylas, M., & Iasonos, S. (2010). Leadership styles and multicultural education approaches: An exploration of their relationship. *International Journal of Leadership in Education, 13*(2), 163-183. doi:10.1080/13603120903386969

INDEX

Key Search Terms In Book:

academic leaders, achievement-oriented leadership, active leadership, affective commitment, autocratic leadership, avoidant leadership, behavioral idealized influence, charismatic leadership, citizenship behaviors, communication styles, contingent reward leadership, developmental leadership, distributive justice, dualistic leadership, effective leadership, empowerment frameworks, exemplary leaders, exploitative innovation, faculty leadership, gender discrimination, hierarchical structure, idealized influence, institutional leadership, job satisfaction, laissez-faire leadership, leadership behaviors, leadership models, leadership theory, management by exception, mentors / protégés, organizational climate / organizational culture, participative leadership, passive/avoidant leadership, professional development, pseudo-transformational leaders, psychological empowerment, realistic leadership, reward and incentive system, scope of influence, shared governance model, structural empowerment, supportive leadership, top-down management style, total quality management (TQM), transactional leadership, transformational leadership

ABOUT THE AUTHOR

Dr. Justin Bateh is an award-winning educator with over 15 years of experience in business, education, and consulting roles. He has taught college courses at the graduate and undergraduate level, and previously held leadership and management roles in the private sector.

He is a tenured faculty member at Florida State College at Jacksonville, in the School of Business and Professional Studies, where he primarily teaches courses in operations and supply chain, applied statistics, and management. His teaching activities are designed to encourage students to think quantitatively about organizational management and leadership problems and issues.

Dr. Bateh has been widely recognized for outstanding contributions to teaching excellence and learning, He is the recipient of the Roland S. Kennedy Endowed Chair for Excellence in Instruction Supporting Business Education, the John & Suanne Roueche Excellence Award, The Clute Institute's Excellence in Research Award, and the ACBSP Teaching Excellence Award.

He completed undergraduate studies at the University of North Florida. He also received an MBA from Nova Southeastern University, a Master's of Science in operations management from University of Arkansas, and a Doctorate of Philosophy in business administration from Walden University. He completed a post-graduate specialization in applied statistics from Penn State University and is also a Certified Six Sigma Black Belt.

Dr. Bateh is the co-author of the textbook, *Using Statistics for Better Business Decisions*, published by Business Expert Press. As a researcher, he has nine papers published in peer-reviewed scholarly journals on management and business. He continues to conduct research in various areas of organizational leadership and management.

He resides in Jacksonville, Florida, and enjoys spending time with his wife and daughter; reading biographical stories of historical world leaders; studying global affairs and international politics; exercising; networking; traveling and learning about different cultures.

You may reach the author via:

drbateh@gmail.com

www.drjustinbateh.com

ABOUT THE BOOK

This book is a must read for administration and human resources staff of colleges and universities who may be having difficulty retaining highly qualified teaching instructors, academic professors, and adjunct faculty staff. The retention of faculty and staff of educational institutions has been of vital concern over the last decade, especially since the economic turmoil of 2008 and the aftermath of the great recession. The increase of online degrees has increased the competitiveness of finding and keeping, qualified and valuable teaching staff. Retention of valuable teaching instructors, including adjunct, part-time, associate, and assistant professors is crucial in the survival and growth of academic institutions, as well as maintenance of accreditation credentialing and standards.

This book focuses on a correlational research study, based on a faculty population in an institution of higher learning in Florida, that examined the relationship between perceived academic administrator leadership styles and the satisfaction of faculty members and transformational, transactional, and passive/avoidant leadership styles of academic administrators, with a dependent variable of job satisfaction for full-time faculty members. Based on a 95% significance level, the researcher identified a significant relationship between the three leadership styles and the academic instructor's job satisfaction, thus an inferred correlational relationship to staff retention.

Using this model, academic leaders are encouraged to refine their leadership styles on the basis of faculty members' indicated preferences to increase and improve academic instructor's retention, as well as their satisfaction in working for the school. Three key recommendations for action were developed. First, senior academic administrators should identify current transformational leaders in their organizations and perhaps use them as mentors to assist in the training and mentorship of current and future leaders. Second, academic administrators should recognize that leadership traits can be learned, and therefore, provide professional development and training opportunities in the areas of transformational leadership for present and future academic leaders. Finally, those who seek leadership positions in academia should become aware of the attributes of an effective higher education administrator, and work to develop an intrinsic understanding of and cultivate a skill-set of transformational leadership characteristics.

www.ingramcontent.com/pod-product-compliance
Lightning Source LLC
Chambersburg PA
CBHW061044110426
42740CB00049B/1809